INVISIBLE:

A PHENOMENOLOGICAL STUDY OF PERSEVERANCE IN BLACK STUDENT-FATHERS IN COMMUNITY COLLEGES

Carl Stokes Jr.

STOKESMEDIA LLC

Copyright © 2020 by Stokes Media, LLC

Cover & Interior Design: Waqar Nadeem

Logo Design: Darrell Stevens

Editor: Jessica Sipos, PhD

All rights reserved. No part of this publication may be reproduced, used, performed, stored in a retrieval system, or transmitted in any form or by any means, electronic, mechanical, photocopying, recording or otherwise without the prior written permission of the author Dr. Carl Stokes Jr., except for critical articles and reviews.

For more information visit:

www.drcarlstokesjr.com

1st edition, December 2020

ISBN – 13: 978-1-7359202-2-1

Printed in the United States of America

DEDICATION

To Hadeen Stokes. This is my opportunity to officially thank you for saving my life. If it were not for you, I would not have a best friend, a beautiful wife, or my Naylani and Nayla. Your light chased away the darkness that consumed my world before I met you. You loved me, believed in me, and single-handedly provided the factors in my life that have inspired and motivated me to keep improving myself. The foundation of our life together began with you standing by my side as I struggled with Black fatherhood. Now, I have written a doctoral dissertation on Black fatherhood. Everything that I am is because of you.

BIOGRAPHICAL SKETCH

Carl Stokes Jr. is currently the chair of the Human Services Department at Erie Community College in Buffalo, New York. Mr. Stokes earned his Associate of Arts in Social Science in 2001, his Bachelor of Science in Sociology from Buffalo State College in 2009, his Master of Social Work in 2013, and his social work license from the New York State Department of Education. He came to St. John Fisher College in the summer of 2018 and began doctoral studies in the Ed.D. Program in Executive Leadership. Mr. Stokes pursued his research in Invisible: A Phenomenological Study of Perseverance in Black Student-Fathers in Community Colleges under the direction of Dr. Guillermo Montes, Dr. Jamie D. Smith, and received the Ed.D. degree in 2020.

ABSTRACT

This transcendental phenomenological study examined how Black fathers' perception of their own and their father's fatherhood impacts persistence in community college. This study interviewed six Black male community college students with children in New York State. The study posed three research questions: (1) How do Black male college students experience fatherhood (from a son's perspective) facilitating or impeding community college completion? (2) How do Black male college students experience their fatherhood (from a father's perspective) facilitating or impeding community college completion? and (3) In the experience of Black male college students, how do community colleges support Black students who are fathers? Findings show that fatherhood acts as a catalyst to community college completion for Black student-fathers, that children are a central motivation for persistence for Black student-fathers, and support systems in community colleges are lacking for Black student-fathers. The six emergent themes included parenting matters, impenetrable lifelong connections, resilience and progression, desire to be living proof, typical unnecessary obstacles, and true acknowledgement and acceptance. Recommendations for practice include recognizing Black student-fathers, implementing support programs specific to Black student-fathers, and actively recruiting Black male faculty and support staff. Recommendations for future research include broadening research nationally, including 4-year institutions, and examining student-fathers of different races.

TABLE OF CONTENTS

Dedication iii

Biographical Sketch iv

Abstract v

Table of Contents vii

List of Tables x

CHAPTER 1: Introduction 11

    Education in the US 11

    Black Americans and Education 16

    Black Male Identity 19

    Theoretical Rationale: Critical Race Theory 23

    Fatherhood 25

    Persistence Research in Higher Education 28

    Problem Statement 32

    Research Purpose and Questions 33

    Potential Implications of the Study 35

    Summary 35

CHAPTER 2: Review of the Literature 37
    Introduction 37
    Black Men in Higher Education 39
    Persistence Models in Higher Education 41
    Factors for Persistence in Community Colleges 45
    Gaps in the Literature and Recommendations 81
    Summary 83
CHAPTER 3: Research Design Methodology 87
    Introduction 87
    Research Questions and Purpose of the Study 88
    Design 89
    Transcendental Phenomenology 90
    Procedure 92
    Participants 93
    Analysis 96
CHAPTER 4: Results 101
    Introduction 101
    Themes 104
    Composite Textural Description 141

    Composite Structural Description 145

    Textural Structural Synthesis 146

    Conclusion 148

CHAPTER 5: Discussion 152

    Introduction 152

    Findings and Implications 154

    Recommendations for Practice 168

    Recommendations for Future Research 175

    Limitations 177

    Conclusion 177

References 182

Appendix A 206

LIST OF TABLES

Item	Title	Page
Table 3.1	Participant Demographics	94
Table 4.1	Research Questions, Themes and Subthemes	102
Table 4.2	Overarching Research Question and Findings	103
Table 4.3	RQ1 – Theme, Subthemes, and Key Concepts	104
Table 4.4	RQ2 – Themes and Key Concepts	119
Table 4.5	RQ3 – Themes, Key Concepts, and Subthemes	132

CHAPTER 1

INTRODUCTION
Education in the US

In the United States, education is viewed as a catalyst to future prosperity, upward mobility, and the overall "American Dream." The American Association of Community Colleges (AACC) reports that the median earnings for full-time workers 25 years and older with less than a high school diploma was approximately $31,315 in 2020 (AACC, 2020). In contrast, the report also states that the average yearly income for full-time workers 25 and older who hold an associate degree is approximately $42,600 per year. Additionally, close to half of all Americans are classified as impoverished (AACC, 2020).

A high percentage of U.S. citizens live in poverty, in some or large part, due to the lack of earned postsecondary education credentials (Carnevale, Rose, & Cheah, 2011; O'Banion, 2013). A 2016 report from Georgetown University supports the importance of a college education for economic stability in the United States after the 2008 recession (Carnevale, Jayasundera, & Gullish, 2016). Since 2010, close to 99% of the jobs added to the economy after the recession went to employees who had postsecondary education.

The lack of earned college degrees often correlates with a lower socioeconomic status, which in turn has links to health problems, unemployment, poverty, and incarceration rates (Mirowsky & Ross, 2003; Palmer, Wood, Dancy, & Strayhorn, 2014; Vuolo, Mortimer, & Staff, 2016). National reports show that some of the links between poverty and health risks are things like lack of access to healthy food, community safety concerns, and stress (Bird et al., 2010). Longitudinal research also suggests that children born into low-income families experience more negative effects over time than their higher-income counterparts (Assari, Thomas, Caldwell, & Mincy, 2017). Further, with education comes more access to steady employment, so there is less chance of falling into petty crime, incarceration, and a resulting criminal record, which affects job opportunities. According to a study on poverty and crime, living in poverty increases likelihood of property crime (Zhao, Feng, & Castillo-Chavez, 2014).

Evidence suggests that social mobility and economic stability are partly contingent upon attaining a postsecondary degree. However, Black males are failing to reap these benefits. According to McFarland et al. (2018), Black men have the lowest percentage of earned/completed secondary degrees in comparison to their White, Latinx and Asian counterparts, despite an increase in postsecondary degrees earned nationwide (McFarland et al., 2018). Between the most recently recorded years of 2013 to 2018, Black males obtained between 12.7% to 13.8% of all associate degrees conferred (National Center for Educational Statistics [NCES], 2019). Additionally, Black students were more likely than the average undergraduate student to leave school without completing a degree within 6 years of initial enrollment (National Urban League, 2014). Therefore, Black males are more likely to suffer the negative outcomes and concomitant risks of lower socioeconomic status.

Quality of life issues are also impacted by educational attainment. For example, certain kinds of work are less menial and taxing on the body. These are often white-collar jobs and professions. Research suggests that white-collar workers report much less musculoskeletal pain than blue-collar workers (Herr et al., 2015). Further, the financial stability afforded by higher-paid, white-collar jobs can protect against economic downturns. People with less wealth are more likely to deplete savings and sell tangible assets to maintain, while those with more wealth can capitalize (Duque, Pilkauskas, & Garfinkel, 2018). Additionally, education can cultivate professionalism that can translate to marketable soft skills like interview skills, how to dress for work, and customer service, to name a few. Indeed, many colleges are "incorporating the softer, noncognitive skills into college-readiness efforts" (Adams, 2012, p. 1).

Studies support the argument that postsecondary education is an important step for achieving beneficial long-term occupational and economic outcomes (Hummer & Lariscy, 2011; McFarland et al., 2018; Schafer et al., 2013). Higher unemployment rates are associated with lower levels of education, lower earnings, and increased criminal activity (McFarland et al., 2018). Links have been established between education and socioeconomic status, as well as potentially between socioeconomic status, health, and incarceration rates (Palmer et al., 2014; Vuolo et al., 2016). Improving rates of earned postsecondary education credentials in Black males can increase their socioeconomic status (Mirowsky & Ross, 2003; Palmer et al., 2014; Vuolo et al., 2016). These improvements can result in lower incarceration rates, which can decrease taxpayer burden. According to data from the Prison Policy Initiative (2017), the annual costs of mass incarceration in the US are well over 100 billion dollars, including state and federal money for prison upkeep, food, and medical care.

Community colleges and access to education. Researchers, such as Melguizo, Kienzl, and Kosiewicz (2013) and O'Banion (2013), recognize the importance of community colleges due to their accessibility for many students who might not otherwise have the opportunity to pursue higher education. Such accessibility allows community colleges to enroll approximately 41% of undergraduate students in the United States (AACC, 2020). Community colleges often serve students from lower socioeconomic backgrounds as well as those who may be less prepared for secondary education (O'Banion, 2013). Community colleges provide students expedient access to the college environment for educational attainment as well as other socioeconomic opportunities (Brand, Pfeffer, & Goldrick-Rab, 2014; Goldrick-Rab, 2010). Additionally, community colleges are vital in developing a skilled workforce (Seidman, 2012). For example, most community colleges offer vocational courses and other training that are not typically a part of a 4-year institution's curriculum, such as automotive technology, brewery operations, and carpentry. Not only are community colleges essential for such training and retraining the U.S. workforce, but they are also essential to positive economic changes such as the infusion of the higher incomes of community college graduates into the economy, more tax revenue, and reduction in the need for services such as Medicare, welfare, and unemployment (AACC, 2014).

BLACK AMERICANS AND EDUCATION

In 1823, Alexander Twilight was the first Black man to receive a bachelor's degree from Middlebury College (Boyd, 2016). Although there was an attempt in 1831 to create a Black college in New Haven, Connecticut, Cheyney University of Pennsylvania, the first Black college was not established until 1837 (Jackson & Jackson, 2016; Moss, 2007). Nonetheless, education is a historical area of disadvantage for Black people in America.

The Black Codes and Jim Crow laws hindered the social, economic, political, and educational progress of Black people in America. During that time, Black Americans' civil rights were ignored and educational opportunities were limited due to segregation and underfunding (Randolph, 2010). Although the Department of Education was created in 1867 to establish effective school systems for the citizenry, schools were legally segregated by race between the *Plessy v. Ferguson* decision in 1896 and *Brown v. Board of Education* decision in 1954 (U.S. Department of Education, 1991; Zamani-Gallaher, 2010).

There is a documented history of Black schools receiving less funding and fewer resources, to the detriment of Black students (Guryan, 2004). The *Brown v. Board of Education* case highlighted that "separate but equal" could not truly be equal as social relationships formed in school are key pieces to the educational process (Moody, 2001). Present-day remnants of those segregated times remain in all levels of education for Black people in America.

Evidence attests to the importance of college credentials in achieving a higher socioeconomic status (Carnevale et al., 2011; O'Banion, 2013). Studies also show that children from single-parent homes have higher rates of impoverishment and lower socioeconomic status (National Fatherhood Initiative, 2018). Socioeconomic status is linked to health, wellness, and behavior in society (Palmer et al., 2014). As stated above, Black males in the United States face multiple challenges due to cultural, social, political, and economic disadvantages created, maintained, and controlled by White power structures (Fornilli, 2018; Levin, Haberler, Walker, & Jackson-Boothby, 2013; Temin, 2017). Empirical studies support the premise that educational attainment is correlated to quality-of-life concerns such as lower health and mortality risks, better socioeconomic attainment, and better access to social and psychological resources (Hummer & Lariscy, 2011; Mirowsky & Ross,

2003; Palmer et al., 2014; Schafer, Wilkenson, & Ferraro, 2013).

Access to higher education has always been a challenge for Black Americans. In fact, education was considered antithetical to a docile enslaved population, and as such, enslaved Black Americans were forbidden to learn to read, upon pain of death, out of fear that literacy would allow them to mobilize against their captors (Conlin, 2015). In the northern states, free Black men were rarely allowed to pursue education beyond primary school. From the Jim Crow era to the present, funding for schools in minority communities has been disparate to what is provided for schools in White communities, with concomitant disparities in skills and knowledge (Jackson & Jackson, 2016).

Only after 1964 were Black Americans allowed to enroll at Primarily White Institutions (PWIs), and even then, faced opprobrium for any effort to matriculate. For example, the elitism of Ivy League schools began with the prestige of their sports programs but soon morphed into a place of grooming for the soon-to-be-powerful (Thelin, 1976). Given this history, the pursuit of higher education in the Black community has been an uphill battle with many obstacles, both personal and institutional, positioned against them (Baumann, 2010). Despite this, many realize the value an advanced degree confers on one's status and economic opportunities and pursue higher education. For many Black students today, community colleges facilitate their access postsecondary education (Wood, Hilton, & Lewis, 2011; Wood & Turner, 2011).

BLACK MALE IDENTITY

Most of the first enslaved Africans who were brought to America in the antebellum South were male (Gutman, 1976). Male slaves were valuable as a source of labor due to their physical strength. Not only did these enslaved men labor in cotton fields, but they also performed tasks such as tending crops, building houses, and plowing fields. In this context, removed from any real participation in the social structures they knew from their homelands in Africa, the first steps toward dehumanization into chattel occurred. Later, when women were also included in the population of enslaved people, many enslaved people formed attachments and even attempts at marriage and families, to the extent they were permitted under the strictures of slavery. When addressing the interpretation of and residual effects on Black manhood during slavery, Foster (2011) recounts the words from a formerly enslaved man named Lewis Clarke. Clarke declared that a slave could not consider himself to be a man because he could not protect his female kin from being assaulted by slave owners and overseers. These types of demoralizing and dehumanizing acts contributed to the deliberate emasculation of Black men (Foster, 2011; Connor & White, 2011). Black enslaved men reported that they did not feel like men during these times of dehumanization because of their inability to protect their families and their lack of identity as fully-realized men (Bellagamba, Greene, Klein, & Brown, 2013; Conlin, 2015; Foster, 2011).

Lack of identity and the feeling of displacement of Black men invoke Maslow's hierarchy of needs (1943), in which he emphasizes the importance of belonging as a basic human need. Maslow states that a man "will hunger for affectionate relations with people in general, namely, for a place in his group, and he will strive with great intensity to achieve this goal" (Maslow, 1943, p. 381). Black American men struggle with their sense of belonging in society (Brooms, 2019). In the context of higher education, researchers such as Strayhorn et al. (2017) qualify a sense of belonging as a perceived sense of community on campus. Historically speaking, pivotal events such as slavery, reconstruction, Jim Crow laws, civil rights movements, drug epidemics, and mass incarceration have caused great hardship and struggle for Black families throughout American history (Du Bois,1903; Connor & White, 2011).

This unrelenting hardship and sense of displacement for Black people lead to what Du Bois (1903) described as the double consciousness of Black people, the notion of looking at oneself through the eyes of others and measuring one's soul through a perspective that sees contempt and pity. Du Bois (1903) states:

The history of the American Negro is the history of this strife,—this longing to attain self-conscious manhood, to merge his double self into a better and truer self. In this merging, he wishes neither of the older selves to be lost ... He simply wishes to make it possible for a man to be both a Negro and an American, without being cursed and spit upon by his fellows, without having the doors of Opportunity closed roughly in his face. (p. 5).

Stereotyping and representation. Du Bois (1903) described the circumstances of Black men being judged and negatively stereotyped during that time. Negative stereotypes about Black men in America as being uneducated and violent persist today (Boyd & Mitchell, 2018). In a 2016 study on the dehumanization and criminalization of Black males, Smiley and Fakunle (2016) write about Blackness being associated with criminality in the United States. They recall former President Barack Obama's reference to Black rioters in Baltimore, Maryland, as "thugs." The former president's response was due to the civil unrest after a Black man by the name of Freddie Gray died in police custody in 2015. During an interview with CNN, former Baltimore

City Council member Carl Stokes (no relation to this researcher) spoke out against the name-calling of citizens (mostly Black) by the former president and members of the media (Smiley & Fakunle, 2016). During the on-air dispute, Stokes pointed out the coded use of the word "thug" in this context. Stokes likened the term "thug" to the term "nigger" (Smiley & Fakunle, 2016).

Smiley and Fakunle (2016) analyzed media coverage of six cases of unarmed Black men who were killed by law enforcement. The cases of Eric Garner, Michael Brown, Jr., Akai Gurley, Tamir Rice, Tony Robinson, and Freddie Gray were examined. They categorized the media portrayals of the victims into four categories: (a) behavior, which was qualified as the actions of the victim at the time of their death and prior to their death; (b) appearance, which was categorized as the physique and style of clothing of the victim at the time of their death; (c) location, which was the geographical area in which the victim's death occurred, as well as where the victim lived; and (d) lifestyle, which included the associated culture of the victim as well as his friends, family, and associates. The stigmatization of Black men in America as dangerous and threatening has created suspicion in social as well as police encounters, and such portrayals that lead to stereotypes can be detrimental to this end (Teasley, Schiele, Adams, & Okilwa, 2018). Media coverage and the concomitant fostering of stereotypes about Black men is related to persistence insofar as such representations of Black males can lead to hostile experiences and unwarranted social opprobrium in ways that can negatively impact their social integration, including in college settings. Cooper et al. (2020) demonstrate how media portrayals lead to negative stereotypes of Black men. Their study examined Black fathers' concerns about how race-related issues and stereotypes impact their children. The study found that negative media portrayals of Black men and absent Black fathers were a key motivation for their positive parenting.

THEORETICAL RATIONALE: CRITICAL RACE THEORY

Critical race theory (CRT) posits that racism is present in everyday interactions and speaks to a power structure that fails to recognize or acknowledge institutional racism (Levin et al., 2013). Originally developed in legal scholarship in the 80s, CRT examines the relationships between race, racism, and power from a social justice standpoint and works to interrogate and challenge the thinking that racial differences are based on the shortcomings of certain races (Teranishi, Behringer, Grey, & Parker, 2009). "Critical race theory was born from a need to further explain and acknowledge inherent racism in society" (Allen, 2016, p.

8). Allen (2016) posits that news outlets' coverage of Black men serves as negative "framing" that contributes to the perpetuation of negative stereotypes of Black men. CRT offers a different perspective on the plight of Black men in America than one that buys into the negative stereotyping promulgated by media portrayals: Black men deal with hardships exacerbated by disadvantages established and enforced by White power structures (Fornili, 2018; Levin et al., 2013; Temin, 2017).

For example, from a CRT perspective, President Richard Nixon's declaration of the War on Drugs in 1971, as well as President Bill Clinton's Violent Crime Control and Law Enforcement Act of 1994, both created unfair disadvantages for minorities (Alexander, 2012; Temin, 2017). The War on Drugs was a major contributor to the mass incarceration of Black males (Fornilli, 2018). The racial significance of mass incarceration becomes apparent when it involves profiling, disproportionate rates of police use of force, disparities in arrests, and the long-term accumulation of arrests for certain racial groups (Alexander, 2012). There is little evidence that drug use and distribution vary significantly by race, yet there are significant disparities in differences in rates of drug arrests by race. Although only 14% of regular users are Black, they have nearly 34% of drug-related arrests (Bobo & Thompson, 2010). Additionally, almost half of drug-related convictions and state prison sentences were given to Blacks, compared to 26% for Whites in the same situation. While some arrests are for distribution, many are due to possession with "intent to use" (Alexander, 2012).

The Violent Crime Control and Law Enforcement Act of 1994 introduced a provision known as the Habitual Offender Law (Three Strikes Law) (McNelis, 2017). This law could bring a life sentence without the possibility of parole to a felon, even if all three convictions are not federal (Sutton, 2013). This firm stance on crime came at a time when the crack cocaine epidemic began to run rampant in the Black community (Alexander, 2012). Due to impoverished conditions, drug distribution and consumption, and institutional racism, many Black men were incarcerated. Increases in the privatization of prisons added an extra element of incentive to make arrests during this time (Alexander, 2012). In speaking about policies such as the War on Drugs, Fornilli (2018) states, "We cannot incarcerate our way out of the alcohol and drug epidemic" (p. 71). Out of the large number of long-term, incarcerated Black males, some were also fathers.

FATHERHOOD

Children growing up with biological fathers in the home are less likely to have behavioral issues, abuse drugs and alcohol, commit crimes, become incarcerated, and drop out of school (Choi & Jackson, 2011; National Fatherhood Initiative, 2018). The benefits of paternal involvement in children are plentiful (National Fatherhood Initiative, 2018). For example, children who have fathers present are less likely to face abuse and neglect and are less likely to commit crimes and become incarcerated (National Fatherhood Initiative, 2018). Past studies have focused on fathers' involvement in children's lives, in general, as well as Black fathers' (or lack thereof) involvement, and the outcomes for their children (Gordon, Nichter, & Henriksen, 2013). Mothers becoming single parents and fathers unable to provide owed child support leads to impoverished children (Duncan, Magnuson, & Votruba-Drzal, 2014).

The colloquial term "deadbeat dad" is used frequently in the Black community. According to Beauchamps, Sazenbacher, Seitz, and Skira (2018), a deadbeat dad is defined as an absent father who does not support his child(ren) financially. Many studies examine challenges Black men face in American society, including their lack of involvement as fathers, broadly and statistically speaking (Beauchamps et al., 2018; Reynolds, 2009; Wilson, Henriksen, Bustamonte, & Irby, 2016). However, some studies primarily focus on the outcomes of children who lack involved fathers (Wilson et al., 2016). When examining absentee fathers in the Black community, historical context provides a deeper understanding of the phenomena.

As discussed above, Black people experience the residual effects of slavery, Jim Crow laws, and other policies and practices that have an adverse effect on this population (Alexander, 2012). For example, economic hardships and increased rates of incarceration in Black males are contributing factors to absentee fathers, leading to low rates of child support payments made by Black fathers (Brito, 2012), all of which can be correlated with low level or quality of education. According to Roberts (2004), the impact of historical inequalities has often led Black families to live in impoverished areas with an oversaturation of law enforcement, which can be correlated to father absence in Black communities. Research from both liberal and conservative perspectives suggests that government policies have contributed to disparities in treatment in Black males (Roberts, 2004; Sowell, 2018).

However, fatherhood is not monolithic, and despite certain challenges described above, a majority of Black men desire to play an intimate role in the rearing of their children (Cooper, 2020). Fatherhood confers purpose and responsibility and, of course, establishes a man as a member of a family system with dependents whom he loves. The value for his family is shared by a majority of Black men, despite ongoing historical practices and policies that separate men from their wives and children, from the capture of Africans for the transatlantic slave trade to Jim Crow laws that led to men working as migrant laborers, or at least, suffering long, underpaid hours, to the present-day policies of mass incarceration (Alexander, 2010) that leave many children without fathers in their homes.

PERSISTENCE RESEARCH IN HIGHER EDUCATION

Although early American higher education instititutions such as Harvard and Yale were established in the 1600s and 1700s, persistence studies in higher education were not conducted until the 1800s (Berger, Ramirez, & Lyon, 2012). The goal of these early colleges and universities was to prepare young men to fill the demand for clergy positions. Over two-thirds of the college graduates during the 1700s became ministers or missionaries (Altbach, Berdahl, & Gumport, 2011).

In the 1800s, focus on both persistence and retention in American higher education was about institutional survival through competition with the education models of other nations (Berger et al., 2012; Demitrou & Schmitz-Sciborski, 2011). For example, German models of higher education emphasized research and specialization in areas other than religious studies

(Altbach et al., 2011). In the United States, the Morrill Land Grant Act of 1862 increased the number of institutions by at least one in each state that offered agricultural and engineering studies (Berger et al., 2012; Cross, 1999; Demitrou & Schmitz-Sciborski, 2011). Student demand was not the catalyst for creating more institutions (Berger et al., 2012; Cross, 1999; Demitrou & Schmitz-Sciborski, 2011). Student enrollment decreased while the number of institutions increased.

In the 1900s, governmental policies, such as the Servicemen's Readjustment Act of 1944 (G.I. Bill), created an increase in enrollment as soldiers returned home from World War II. (Berger et al., 2012; Smith, Ralph, LaFayette, & Finley, 2016; Zamani-Gallaher, 2010). The primary purpose of the G.I. Bill was to assist veterans in acquiring the skills necessary to readjust to civilian life and expand the middle class (Berger et al., 2012; Zamani-Gallaher, 2010). However, Black veterans were not able to take advantage of these benefits as the G.I. Bill, as White supremacist politics led to these benefits distributed almost unilaterally to White veterans (Zamani-Gallaher, 2010).

An increased focus on persistence occurred during the 1960s due to large numbers of minority students enrolling in higher education (Astin, 1985; Berger et al., 2012). The Civil Rights Act of 1964 and the Higher

Education Act of 1965 were also passed during that time (Berger et al., 2012; Smith et al., 2016; Zamani-Gallaher, 2010). These social and legislative movements contributed to the growth of racial and ethnic minorities on college campuses due to the protections offered to Black people and other minorities from discrimination as well as the financial strengthening of HBCUs (Berger et al., 2012; Zamani-Gallaher, 2010).

During the 20th century, college student persistence theories in the United States began to emerge (Berger et al., 2012). Studies such as those of Spady (1970), Tinto (1975), and Bean and Metzner (1985) are highly cited. Tinto's (1975) model of student departure added to Spady's (1970) concepts of social and academic integration in higher education institutions (Bean & Metzner, 1985; Mason, 1994; Metz, 2004; Wood 2013). Spady's (1970) study on dropouts from higher education was one of the most influential and widely accepted studies in the persistence literature (Bean & Metzner, 1985). Tinto (1975) credited Spady (1970) for being the first person to apply Durkheim's 1897 theory of suicide, which postulated that suicide is more likely to occur in individuals who are not well integrated into society, to problems with dropouts insofar as students might drop out if they were not sufficiently integrated into their educational settings (Abrutyn & Miller, 2014; Durkheim, 2005; Spady, 1970; Thibodeau & Lachaud, 2016; Tinto, 1975).

Spady's (1970) undergraduate dropout process model examined how academic and social variables impacted student persistence. Tinto's (1975, 1993) model of student departure also investigated the role of social and academic integration while focusing more on traditional students in 4-year settings (Aljohani, 2016; Demitrou & Schmitz-Sciborski, 2011; Metz, 2004). Astin's (1984) model of student involvement worked under the premise that student involvement, or lack thereof, in college life were the determining factors of departure. Bean and Metzner's (1985) model of non-traditional student attrition focused on non-traditional students. Mason's (1998) persistence model for African American male, urban, community college students looked at Black men at community colleges.

Mason (1998) took background variables, academic variables, and environmental variables into account to determine why Black male students persist in community colleges utilizing a strengths-based approach to examine why students persist, rather than trying to determine why students leave college, as Tinto (1993) and Bean and Metzner (1985) did. Mason (1998) found that outside encouragement (typically mothers) was a significant factor (Mason, 1998). This study looked deeper into Mason's (1998) outside encouragement variable as a factor of fatherhood in the persistence of Black males in community colleges. Wood and Harris's (2012) model continued in the tradition of Mason's (1998) model to examine the persistence of Black males in community colleges.

PROBLEM STATEMENT

This study integrates the intersections of higher education, fatherhood, and being a Black man in the United States. Given the established position of Black men as the lowest ranking in postsecondary degree attainment (McFarland et al., 2018) and the role of community colleges in providing access to postsecondary education for Black students (Wood, 2011; Wood & Turner, 2011), an increased interest in Black male student persistence has emerged in education studies (Harper, 2012). Numerous studies have investigated disparities in the achievement of Black males and achievement in other male groups (Strayhorn, 2012; Wood & Williams, 2013), as well as disparities in Black males being raised without the support of a father (Orrock & Clark, 2018; Strayhorn, Hilton, & Bonner, 2017; Wood & Williams, 2013).

However, limited research addresses the advantages and disadvantages of how paternal involvement impacts fathers' educational goals and persistence in community college settings, and no studies investigate how fatherhood impacts persistence in Black student-fathers in community college settings. Persistence literature on Black male students at community colleges is minimal compared to the persistence literature on traditional students at 4-year institutions (Bush & Bush, 2010; Palmer et al., 2014), and current research on persistence in higher education does not fully reflect Black student-fathers' perceptions and experiences about how fatherhood (their own and their fathers') affects community college completion. This study endeavors to fill this gap in the literature, especially given the crucial role community colleges play in the pursuit of higher education for Black men.

RESEARCH PURPOSE AND QUESTIONS

The purpose of this study was to gain a better understanding of Black student-fathers in community colleges, their experiences of any impact that fatherhood has, or has had, on their persistence toward completing their studies. The study also sought to learn more about whether Black student-fathers feel supported in community colleges, and how community colleges support their success. The study also aimed to give Black student-fathers a voice. The overarching research question was: How do Black males perceive fatherhood (their own, and their father's), and how does it impact their persistence in community college?

The following research questions guided the study:

1. How do Black male college students experience fatherhood (from a son's perspective) facilitating or impeding community college completion?

2. How do Black male college students experience their fatherhood (from a father's perspective) facilitating or impeding community college completion?

3. In the experience of Black male college students, how do community colleges support Black students who are fathers?

Persistence theory was used to inform explanations as to why students do not complete secondary education programs (Astin, 1984; Mason, 1998; Spady, 1970; Tinto, 1975, 1993;). Wood and Harris's (2012) five domains model served as a guide for the literature review as it focuses on the persistence of Black males in community colleges. Using persistence theory to inform the study served as a starting point to explore factors related to student success. This was due in part to a focus on departure and dropout behavior, and the lack of literature exploring why Black male students stay in college and earn certificates and degrees (Bush & Bush, 2010; Harper, 2012; Palmer et al., 2014). The study population was comprised of Black student-fathers in community colleges. The participants had between one and four children, were both employed and unemployed, and were pursuing different courses of study.

POTENTIAL IMPLICATIONS OF THE STUDY

According to Palmer et al. (2014) and Vuolo et al. (2016), the lack of earned college degrees correlates to lower socioeconomic status, which in turn has links to health concerns, poverty, and incarceration rates. Additionally, economists such as Williams (1996) and Sowell (2018) state that children from fatherless homes are more likely to suffer from poverty, have behavioral problems, drop out of school, join gangs, commit crimes, and become incarcerated. If fatherhood and postsecondary degree attainment play such a vital role in the economics, behavior, and health of not only the men in question, but their children, and by extension, their families and communities, a deeper look into these issues is critical both for local communities in question as well as society at large.

SUMMARY

Higher education, Black male identity, and fatherhood are the central concerns of this study. The historical challenges against education at all levels for

Black Americans was articulated, as well as other structural policies that challenge educational achievement and persistence. Black men's success in men's success in community college, in general, provides an opportunity to break down some stereotypes about Black men as well as to chip away at disparities between Black males and other groups. Specifically giving voice to Black student-fathers in community colleges, as this study does, fosters a better understanding of the role that fatherhood has, or has had, on their persistence toward completing their studies. The study also aimed to learn more about potential motivations or challenges Black student-fathers face in community colleges and what community colleges do or do not do to support their success, and how institutional support may facilitate academic achievement for this population.

Chapter 2 presents a review of the literature. Chapter 3 describes the study methodology and Chapter 4 presents the findings. Chapter 5 discusses the findings and implications of this study and offers recomendations for practice and future research.

CHAPTER 2

REVIEW OF THE LITERATURE

INTRODUCTION

This chapter presents an overview of the empirical studies that focus on the experiences of Black male students in higher education and describes how persistence theory is used to frame this study. As stated in Chapter 1, this study utilized a three-pronged approach: the interstices between higher education, fatherhood, and being a Black man in the United States. To organize the literature, Chapter 2 discusses foundational models of persistence, followed by culturally specific models. This chapter then presents relevant literature about Black males in higher education through Wood and Harris's (2012) five domains model, which includes: (a) noncognitive domain, (b) environmental domain, (c) academic domain, (d) institutional domain, and (e) social domain. This model is the only comprehensive model that focuses on literature specific to Black male success in community colleges.

Research shows that Black male persistence is challenged in 2-year colleges (Vasquez-Urias & Wood, 2014). Studies such as Strayhorn (2014) and Wood and Harrison (2014) examine Black male student success in postsecondary education. Studies such as those of Beauchamp et al. (2018) and Allen (2016) examine outcomes of Black males as they pertain to their relationships with fatherhood. Although these studies investigate these topics, there is a lack of studies that examine the relationship between how Black fathers perceive fatherhood (their own and their father's) and how these perceptions impact their persistence in community college settings. This review presents the literature on Black fatherhood and the literature on the outcomes of Black males in higher education, with the goal of informing and contextualizing the findings of this dissertation study.

BLACK MEN IN HIGHER EDUCATION

Research on the topic of Black males in higher education has yielded an abundance of data and suggestions for strategies aimed toward improving persistence. A number of empirical studies have examined Black males in higher education in settings such as Predominantly White Institutions (PWI) and Historically Black Colleges and Universities (HBCU) (Palmer et al., 2014). Other studies on Black males in higher education investigate graduate and undergraduate studies, as well as students' levels of college preparedness. According to the literature, there are many variables related to the persistence of Black male students in pursuing higher education (Harris & Wood, 2013; Mason, 1998; Strayhorn, 2014; Wood & Harrison, 2014).

Harris and Wood's (2013) review addressed Black male success in community college settings. This review differs in a few ways. First, Harris and Wood's (2013) review examined the literature between the years of 1998 and 2012, whereas this review examines the literature since 2013. Second, they were able to implement their own previously developed framework (the five domains model) in their literature review (Harris & Wood, 2012; Wood & Harris, 2016). Third, this review examines the literature on Black males in community colleges and 4-year colleges, whereas Harris and Wood (2013) only reviewed the literature related to Black males in community colleges. Moreover, in the context of Black students in higher education, this review includes studies that look at both male and female students The approach of this review provides a broader scope for the empirical literature on Black males in higher education. Further, the extant literature on Black males in community colleges is not extensive (Bush & Bush, 2010; Palmer, 2014) and thus, a more updated and comprehensive review of the literature on Black males in higher education is of importance to the topic.

Conversely, this review shares similarities to Harris and Wood's (2013) review. First, the premise of this review is to contribute to the research on Black males in higher education. Second, this review also uses Wood and Harris's (2012) five domains model of Black male student success as a guide to organizing this literature review. Although the five domains model was created to describe the experiences of Black male students in community college settings, this review uses the model to evaluate the literature on Black males in undergraduate programs, in general. As previously stated, the five domains included in this model are the noncognitive, environmental, academic, institutional, and social domains (Harris & Wood, 2016; Wood & Harris, 2012). A meta-analysis of the literature found the factors for Black male success in higher education to be self-efficacy, social support, academic support, and male role models.

These factors are presented through the applicable domains of the five domains model (Wood & Harris, 2013; Harris and Wood, 2016).

This review serves as a contribution to the literature on Black male students in community colleges. This review also explores the social variables of existing literature on Black male persistence in community college settings. Within the theme of social variables described in the extant literature, few studies have closely examined the role of fatherhood on the perspectives of Black male student-father persistence in higher education.

PERSISTENCE MODELS IN HIGHER EDUCATION

Several researchers have offered initial contributions to the college retention and attrition literature (Astin, 1975; Bean, 1983; Bean & Metzner, 1985; Mason, 1998; Pascarella, 1980; Spady, 1970; Tinto, 1975, 1993). Although not the first, Tinto's (1975) model of student integration is considered the beginning of modern college retention studies (Demetriou & Schmitz-Sciborski, 2011). Tinto (1975) focused on 4-year college students, hypothesizing that students are less likely to graduate if they are not socially integrated into the campus community (Demetriou & Schmitz-Sciborski,

2011). Between 1975 and 1993, Tinto's (1975) model was heavily critiqued and revised by himself and by other researchers (Cabrera et al., 1993; Pascarella & Terenzini, 1983; Tinto, 1988). Tinto modified and updated his original work from this period (Tinto, 1993).

Foundational models. Based on the analysis of several seminal works (Bean, 1980; Bean & Metzner, 1985; Mason, 1998), Tinto's (1975) model is one of the most important frameworks in student persistence in higher education. Tinto's (1993) revised model of institutional departure postulated that both academic and social systems that comprise college settings. For students to persist through the goal of graduation, they must be fully integrated into both systems (Tinto, 1975, 1993). Intellectual development and grade point average fall under the academic system, whereas student involvement with peers and faculty are included in the social system. Tinto's model posits that academic and student integration, or lack thereof are determining factors for departure from the institution.

Even though considered a seminal study, several criticisms of Tinto's model arose (Cabrera et al., 1992; Longwell-Grice & Longwell-Grice, 2007; Pascarella & Terenzini, 1979, 1980, 1983, 1991). One criticism of the model is that it only focused on 4-year institutions (Metz, 2004). Another criticism is that the model lacked generalizability because the focus was on traditional students (Tierney, 1992). Additionnally, minority groups such as people with disabilities, LGBTQ, different racial groups, or any other groups considered to be at risk of dropping out are not mentioned (Metz, 2004). An exclusive look at Black students in higher education was also not considered in Tinto's (1975, 1993) model.

Whereas Tinto's (1975, 1993) models focused on students' social withdrawal, Bean and Metzger's (1985) non-traditional undergraduate student attrition model compared student departure to employee turnover. Bean and Metzner (1985) highlighted the lack of studies focusing on nontraditional undergraduate students and turned their attention toward commuter students in contrast with Tinto (1975), who focused on traditional students who lived on college campuses. Bean and Metzner (1985) posited that students are impacted more by environmental factors such as family and other outside commitments, as opposed to individual attributes. Environmental variables included factors such as work hours, outside encouragement, lack of finances, transfer opportunities, and family responsibilities (Bean & Metzner, 1985).

Bean and Metzner's (1985) non-traditional undergraduate student attrition model includes the factors of academic performance, background, demographic and environmental variables, and intent to leave. They argue that academic performance variables suggest that students with lower academic performance were more likely to withdraw. Student intention to leave is "expected to be influenced primarily by the psychological outcomes but also by the academic variables" (Bean & Metzner, 1985, p. 490). In summary, individual background, variables such as student high school achievement, and educational goals influence student persistence.

Culturally specific models. Disparities in college completion rates between Black males and other ethnic groups documented in seminal works on Black male persistence in higher education remain valid (Glenn, 2003; Mason, 1998). For example, even with overall increases in postsecondary degree attainment among various racial and ethnic groups, Black males remain among the lowest achieving (Musu-Gillette et al., 2017). Within 6 years, 69% of Asian students graduate with a 4-year degree, Latinx students graduate at 69%, Whites graduate at 62%, and Black students come in at the lowest percentage at 39% (Anumba, 2015).

There is also a disparity between college completion rates of Black women and Black men. As reported by Musu-Gillette et al. (2017), even though females graduated more than males across all racial and ethnic groups, the gap between male and female undergraduates was the widest among Black students. When separated by gender, 34% of Black males graduate with a bachelor's degree after 6 years versus 66% for Black females (Anumba, 2015).

A consistent theme within the literature on Black males in higher education is that Black males face challenges such as insecurity in their identity, racism, and lack of support (Glenn, 2003; Mason, 1998).

FACTORS FOR PERSISTENCE IN COMMUNITY COLLEGES

The seminal work on persistence in Black males is Mason's (1998) Chicago-based study, which focused on African American, male, urban community-college students. The study surveyed four specific groups of Black male students: (a) students who failed to complete the fall semester; (b) students who completed the fall semester; (c) students who completed the fall semester and started back again in the spring semester; and (d) students who completed both the fall and spring semesters. Background variables, academic variables, and environmental variables from previously developed retention/attrition models were considered in Mason's (1998) research. Elaborating on earlier persistence literature (Astin, 1975; Bean, 1983; Bean & Metzner, 1985; Pascarella, 1980; Spady, 1970; Tinto, 1975, 1993), Mason (1998) looked explicitly at persistence factors for these Black males in community college settings, using a mixed-methods study that found that variables contributing to persistence were the helplessness/hopelessness factor, outside encouragement, education goals, and utility.

Through survey data and interviews, Mason (1998) found four key variables of persistence in Black males in community college settings. The first variable is the helplessness/hopelessness factor. This is described as "the belief of many students that no matter what they did or achieved, they would not get a job or be successful" (Mason, 1998, p. 758). The second variable in Mason's (1988) study is outside encouragement. Outside encouragement is described as the likelihood for a student to persist when they had more support from outside from a close girlfriend, wife, or mother (Mason, 1998). The third factor is educational goals, which are described as the more deeply and clearly the students thought about what they wanted to achieve, the more likely they were to persist (Mason, 1998). The fourth key variable is utility, which is described as the student's belief that the academic program would provide future benefits.

Five domains model. Mason's (1998) work on Black males in community college settings was continued by Wood and Harris (2012) and Harris and Wood (2016). In the original five domains model, Wood and Harris (2012) identified five key themes (domains) that impact the success outcomes of Black male students in higher education. They expanded the five domains model to produce the socio-ecological model (SEO) (Harris & Wood, 2016). It should be noted that the five domains model was chosen to organize this literature review because the model solely focuses on Black male students in community colleges as opposed to the SEO model, which includes men of color other than Black (Harris & Wood, 2016). The literature in this review is guided and presented within the noncognitive domain, the academic domain, the environmental domain, the institutional domain, and the social domain (Wood & Harris, 2012). The following sections will go into the details of this model.

The noncognitive domain. The noncognitive domain is comprised of the emotional responses to social interactions based on a person-in-environment context (Wood & Harris, 2012; Harris & Wood, 2016). The person-in-environment concept is based on categorizing an individual's interpersonal, environmental, mental, and physical concerns (Karls, Lowery, Mattaini, & Wandrei, 1997). Psychosocial variables such as action control, degree utility, locus of control, and self-efficacy fall under the noncognitive domain (Wood & Harris, 2012; Harris & Wood, 2016). Factors for persistence within the literature on Black males in college within the noncognitive domain are reviewed under the categories of self-efficacy and impacts on identity.

Self-efficacy as a factor for persistence. Bandura (1997) states that people's beliefs about their capabilities can positively influence their behaviors. In the context of Black male students, Harris & Wood (2013) define self-efficacy as "students' confidence and perceived ability to complete academic coursework successfully" (p. 334). When speaking about factors that influence Black male student achievement in college, Reid (2013) found that students who reported high self-efficacy, high levels of institutional integration, and positive racial identity earned better grades in college.

Reid's (2013) quantitative study examined 190 Black males from five research universities. It should be noted that a sixth university was willing to participate but was not selected due to not being a research university (Reid, 2013). While not based on qualitative data from community colleges, this study is relevant due to the highlighted experiences of Black males in higher education. Participants in Reid's (2013) study, on average, had the following characteristics: (a) nearly finished with their junior year, (b) majoring in a STEM discipline, (c) earning a grade point average of 2.97, (d) came to the institution with a B+ average, (e) had an SAT score of about 1240, (f) had parents who attended some college, and (g) had an average family income between $25,000-$50,000.

The study utilized three separate instruments to form one web-based questionnaire (Reid, 2013). The first instrument was the Self-Efficacy for Academic Milestone Scale (AMS) (Lent, Brown, & Larkin 1986). This instrument rated students' confidence in their ability to achieve specific academic goals. The second instrument used was a condensed version of the Black Racial Identity Attitude Scale (RIAS-B) (Helms, 1990; Parham & Helms, 1981). The RIAS-B is a revision of the Racial Identity Attitude Scale (RIAS) (Parham & Helms, 1981). This scale measures attitudes that reflect the stages of Black identity development originally proposed by Cross, Parham, and Helms (1991). The stages in the scale are pre-encounter, encounter, immersion/emersion, internalization, and internalization/commitment. The third instrument used by Reid (2013) was the Institutional Integration scale (IIS) (Pascarella & Terenzini, 1980). This scale measures the five facets of institutional integration: (a) peer-group relations, (b) informal relations with faculty, (c) faculty concern for teaching and student development, (d) academic and intellectual development, and (e) institutional/goal commitment (Pascarella & Terenzini, 1980).

Reid's (2013) findings are consistent with the study on Black male preparation for college and success by Strayhorn (2015). This mixed-methods study examined factors that promote Black male student success in college. Similar to Reid (2013), Strayhorn (2015) examined Black male students in STEM disciplines. However, participants in the Strayhorn (2015) sample consisted of students who also majored in other fields such as business, education, and social sciences.

Contrary to Reid's (2013) study, Strayhorn (2015) conducted a longitudinal study with 140 full-time students who were enrolled at large, public HBCUs or PWIs. The participants in the Strayhorn (2015) study were also from urban neighborhoods. Like Reid (2013), Strayhorn (2015) found that self-efficacy was a major factor in influencing Black males' preparation and success in college. What differed in Strayhorn's (2015) finding was the pre-college self-efficacy was highlighted as a significant factor in Black male student success. In speaking on the importance of academic self-efficacy, participants used words and phrases like "confidence," endurance," and "feel like I can do it" to describe the internal force that motivates them to achieve academically, persist in college despite setbacks, and major in STEM fields where they feel like "the only one" or "a speck in a sea of Whiteness" (Strayhorn, 2015, p. 54).

Impacts on identity as a factor for persistence. Black men, like all people, have internal and external identities (Cooper, 2013), which are shaped by a myriad of factors, public and private, personal, and communal. Black males, in particular, have faced particular challenges in the shaping of their self-identities, owing to negative public representations and stereotypes, which have oftentimes been internalized, or at the least, demand a personal resistance to avoid succumbing to a negative self-identity after relentless onslaughts of racist depictions in the public imagination. For example, historical and cultural policies such as the War on Drugs have led to the mass incarceration of Black males (Alexander, 2012; Cooper, 2013). These incarceration rates have been a contributing factor toward the criminal stereotype of Black males. Overcoming such negative stereotypes often complicates self-identity in Black males. Researchers, such as Cross et al. (1991), suggest that the identity of Black men goes through a five-stage process (Nigrescence model) that consists of (a) pre-encounter, (b) encounter, (c) immersion/emersion, (d) internalization, and (e) internalization/commitment. Pre-encounter involves the range of how important race is to a person. The range is from race neutrality to race negative. The encounter stage includes which attitudes about race are challenged by life events that may cause a person to transform his conceptualizations of identity. The immersion/emersion stage is when a person's racial attitudes are forgotten to identify with Black culture. Internalization is when a person overcomes identity conflicts and adopts a positive Black identity. The internalization/commitment stage is when the person is comfortable and fully committed to the Black experience. Black men start as children with a neutral to negative attitude about their race, which continues, or can be transformed to a positive one by life experiences (Cross et al., 1991).

The environmental domain. Wood and Harris (2012) and Harris and Wood (2016) acknowledge that commitments outside of college obligations can take time and energy away from a student's studies. For example, variables such as finances, transportation, family responsibilities, and stressful life events are considered to fall under the environmental domain (Wood & Harris, 2012; Harris & Wood, 2016). However, Mason (1998) posits a different take on what constitutes environmental variables. While Mason (1998) includes finances and family responsibilities, he also includes other key variables. Many environmental variables are negative in Mason's view due to the helplessness/hopelessness factor, which is the notion that a student truly believes that he would fail to be successful regardless of how hard he tries. Factors for persistence within the literature on Black males in college within the environmental domain are reviewed below under the categories of social support and male role models. Indeed, Mason (1998) considers environmental variables to be among the most complex sets of variables when dealing with Black males in higher education. "The main discriminating factor appears to be how each student perceives his environment" (Mason, 1998, p. 757). Consistent with Wood and Harris (2012) and Harris and Wood (2016), family responsibilities and employment are key variables under the paradigm of environment, but so are levels of helplessness/hopelessness and outside encouragement (Mason, 1998).

As stated above, not all environmental variables are categorized as factors that distract from educational focus. When referring to outside encouragement, Mason (1998) states that the more support a student has (typically, mothers, girlfriends, and wives), the more likely he is to persist in his studies. Outside encouragement by way of overall social support is, arguably, a significant factor in the persistence of Black males in higher education. Under the umbrella of the environmental domain, social support, male role models, on-campus race relations, and community expectations are factors for persistence in Black men pursuing higher education.

Social support as a factor for persistence. One study on Black males successfully earning postsecondary degrees focused on retention and persistence among Black males in 4-year institutions in California

(Anumba, 2015). The purpose of the study was to identify the factors of persistence among Black males 4-year schools in California. Anumba (2015) proposed that various networks of support systems provide Black males with the social and cultural capital that is critical to their persistence. The suggested networks of support to facilitate success in college for Black males were identified as family, faculty, and staff.

In this study, Anumba (2015) collected data from Black male students who were the first in their family to attend college and who completed at least 2 years at the same 4-year institution. The author utilized purposeful sampling to select participants, with snowball sampling to recruit additional participants. The data from nine participants were analyzed using Moustakas' (1994) transcendental phenomenological approach and Finlay's (2013) data immersion.

Similar to other studies reviewed here, such as Brooks (2015) and Holliday and Strange (2013), Anumba (2015) used a qualitative design to provide opportunities to hear the voices of the participants, which is appropriate for gaining a deeper understanding of Black males' persistence in higher education. For successful outcomes, themes that emerged from the interviews in the study were self-determination, time management, remaining focused, and establishing networks and connections. A notable finding that emerged from the data was that success in college is a group effort as opposed to an individual one. Although the study was conducted at a 4-year institution, the insights on the role of support for Black males in higher education are applicable to other educational contexts.

A further contribution to the research and empirical support for assessing the role of support systems of Black males in higher education comes from Brooks (2015). While Anumba (2015) utilized a qualitative study to examine Black males through the lens of CRT, Brooks (2015) examined both Black males and Black females through the lens of family life course theory. The study's objective was to examine how impactful family structure and support were on Black student persistence. Brooks (2015) sought to understand how Black college students described their family dynamics and how their move from home to college impacted their family relationships.

Brooks (2015) collected data from nine Black female and five Black male participants who were beyond their second year at an HBCU in the South. The participants' ages ranged from 20 to 23 years old and they were interviewed face to face. Four participants were in their junior year and 10 participants were in their senior year. Pseudonyms were used instead of participant' real names, and identifying markers were redacted from documentation in Brooks' (2015) study.

Similar to Anumba (2015), Brooks (2015) highlighted the importance of support in the higher education endeavors of Black students. However, Brooks (2015) found that participants had a different way of defining family. Participants in Brooks' (2015) study were made up of family members who did not live in the home, while participants in Anumba's (2015) study only cited immediate family members in the household. A significant factor in the Brooks (2015) study was that all participants except one had either a mother or a father who had attended college. This is in contrast to the participants in Anumba's (2015) study in that eight of the 9 participants' family members lacked a college education. Similarly, participants in both studies reported that the support of their family was a critical part of their persistence in college (Anumba, 2015; Brooks, 2015).

Each participant in Brooks' (2015) study reported that their family members instilled in them the value of a college education from an early age. In some form during the interview, the concepts of expectations and pride were discussed by every participant. Several participants used financial struggles that their families experienced as motivation to attend college in order to obtain gainful employment and to help their families financially. For nine of the participants, family members expected them to attend college. The lone participant who did not have a mother or father who attended college reported that attending college was not optional from a personal perspective because she endured financial hardships that came from her parents' lack of college education.

Participants in the Brooks (2015) study also expressed that their relationships with immediate family members strengthened after they officially became college students. Some participants stated that family members helped by offering assistance and encouragement through things like help with tuition, household items for their dorms, and visits. Some participants reported that their once-strained family relationships improved due to having time apart from one another (Brooks, 2015).

Brooks' (2015) study was different from other studies in this review in two notable ways. First, Brooks (2015) qualitatively assessed both Black male and female participants' perspectives, whereas studies such as Anumba (2015) and Strayhorn et al. (2017), described below, only assessed Black males. Second, Brooks (2015) offered data that suggests that students' motivation to succeed came from wanting to venture out on their own to avoid being a financial burden on their families, as well as to be a role model for other family members. The theme of family was consistent with other studies.

More recent empirical support for family and other support systems in relation to Black male persistence in higher education comes from the work of Strayhorn et al. (2017). The purpose of their study was to identify success factors for persistence in Black men in public, urban institutions. The authors posited that background traits, academic readiness, access that higher education institutions provide, support systems, and tight-knit community connections are key to Black male student persistence. This mixed-methods study used secondary analysis of previously obtained data through the Integrated Postsecondary Education Data System (IPEDS), as well as informal interviews with Black male college students who attended public, urban institutions.

As mentioned above, quantitative data are gathered annually by the NCES from institutions that participate in student aid programs (Title VI) (Strayhorn et al., 2017). IPEDS data consists of survey components such as student enrollment, financial aid, and completion that are collected over the fall, winter, and spring of each year. Although Strayhorn et al. (2017) do not mention a theory in the study, there is a reference to Tinto's (1993) definition of "retention" in reviewing the data.

Data were collected through informal, semi-structured, face-to-face interviews. Strayhorn et al. (2017) describe the interview participants as being made up of a "fairly small" convenience sample of

Black male participants who attended large, public institutions. The vague description of the participants in the qualitative portion of the study differs from the more detailed descriptions of the participants in the Anumba (2015) and Brooks (2015) studies. Like Anumba (2015) and Brooks (2015), Strayhorn et al. (2017) inquired about the social aspect of students' college experiences. However, the inquiry about the academic experiences of the participants is unique to the Strayhorn et al. (2017) study.

Different groups were tested using "z tests" to estimate differences between retention rates at HBCUs and PWIs. Strayhorn et al. (2017) used data from a Strayhorn (2008) study. The data were analyzed using Strauss and Corbin's (1998) method of comparison. The data were categorized and combined through related themes. Categories that were not related were utilized as independent units.

The results of this mixed-methods study offer suggestions on two separate dynamics (enrollment and persistence) when looking at the success of Black males through comparison of HBCUs and PWIs. Through the qualitative data, the findings suggest that students' SAT and ACT scores at PWIs are higher than their entrance exam scores at HBCUs. Qualitative findings also suggest that students pay less to attend HBCUs than PWIs. The espoused beliefs and values that emerged from the qualitative data are that available supports, access, and close community relationships are the keys to success in Black males (Strayhorn et al., 2017). The connection between the qualitative and quantitative approach in the Strayhorn et al. (2017) study is significant, as test scores and higher tuition provide an empirical measurement of college issues that were mentioned by participants in the qualitative portion of the study. The authors expand on the body of literature by quantitatively assessing Black male students' experience in college persistence, which enabled the participants' voices to be triangulated in the quantitative data collected. A common theme between Anumba (2015), Brooks (2015), and Strayhorn et al. (2017) is that support is essential to Black male success in college. In terms of support, Anumba (2015) found that social and academic support are factors. Brooks (2015) specifically focused on family support as a success factor. Meanwhile, Strayhorn et al.'s (2017) findings regarding support for Black students' experience with persistence in college speak about support more in terms of on-campus services such as counseling, tutoring, and other academic supports as factors for success. Together, these findings bring into relief the salient issues affecting Black men who pursue higher education.

In addition to the theme of support as essential to Black male persistence in higher education, Anumba

(2015), Brooks (2015), Strayhorn et al. (2017), and Rhoden (2017) also highlights the importance of trust. Rhoden's (2017) study found that trust (trust in themselves, others, and the institution) are significant factors in the academic success of Black males. Similar to Orrock and Clark (2018) and Wood and Harrison (2014), Rhoden's (2017) study examined Black male high school students to discover what factors in the precollegiate years impact college persistence. The study is unique in that that the participants were selected in high school, but were interviewed during their second year of college, and is thus able to demonstrate how high school development may have impacted participants' current college success.

In Rhoden's (2017) study, 10 students participated in semi-structured interviews. The themes that emerged were that trust in themselves, trust in others, and trust in the institution are the significant factors pertaining to college persistence. The idea of trust in others included teachers (high school), faculty (college), and peers (both). These ideas are consistent with the theme of academic support in various studies (Knaggs, Sondergeld, & Schardt, 2015; Wood, 2014; Wood & Williams, 2013). Whether the studies are qualitative or quantitative in design, social support by way of relationships is a constant in the research on Black male persistence in higher education. This is also consistent with Harris and Wood (2013) as one of the major findings in the literature review. The following section will explore factors for persistence within the literature on Black males in college within the environmental domain under the category of male role models.

Male role models as a factor for persistence. While the studies described above briefly mention the role of background variables when considering Black males in higher education settings, Orrock and Clark (2018) approached background variables in a different context. According to the U.S. Census Bureau (2016), Black children under the age of 18 who live at home with both parents is 38.7% compared to 74.3% for White children.

Although Orrock and Clark (2018) focus on family support, similar to Anumba (2015), Brooks (2015), Strayhorn et al. (2017), and Wood and Williams (2013), this study concentrates on the risk factor of single-parent family systems. The purpose of the Orrock and Clark (2018) study was to examine contributing factors for academic success in Black males from at-risk populations. At-risk included Black male students between the ages of 16 and 18 who were on track to graduate on time, were considered low socioeconomic status, and were being raised by a single mother (Orrock & Clark, 2018). The authors approached the study with an ecological systems perspective (Brofenbrenner, 1996). Different from the research above, this qualitative study focused on achievement-minded Black males from one rural and one urban high school in at-risk environments in the southeast United Stats. Participants were selected through the school district's database. Six in-person interviews were conducted with willing participants for about an hour each.

Orrock and Clark (2018) state, "the dynamics of having a single parent household have many disadvantages and increases stress for the family" (p. 1015). The authors highlight the possibility that Black males being raised by a single mother may have less access to positive male role models. This lack of positive role models can, in turn, have adverse effects such as lowered self-esteem, increased chance of joining negative peer groups, and lowered confidence in terms of academics (Orrock & Clark, 2018). Data were analyzed through inductive reasoning to assist with the development of themes. Triangulation was utilized, and the agreed-upon themes were community support belonging to a school community, outreach and family values, and positive self-concept.

Due to participants being raised in households with single mothers, the family theme in Orrock and Clark (2018) differed from the family themes in Anumba (2015), Brooks (2015), Strayhorn et al., (2017), and Wood and Williams (2013) by presenting and discussing subcategories of messages of influence from parents, grandparents, and cousins largely due to these family members' support of the single mother. Additionally, the added elements of participants' ages ranging from 16 to 18 years old appeared to impact participants' strong opinions on community support. Participants in Orrock and Clark (2018) emphasized the value of neighbors, coaches, and other family members, all of which articulated fondness for male figures in their families. Messages of influence from parents, grandparents, and cousins mirrored the theme of family expectations of the participants demonstrated in the Brooks (2015) study. The difference between the family influence theme in the two studies is that Wood and Williams's (2013) participants were males, while Brooks's (2015) study participants were both male and female.

Orrock and Clark (2018) address a widely acknowledged fact that many Black males are raised by single mothers, and as such, may lack positive male role models. Supporting the Orrock and Clark (2018) study, Holliday and Strange's (2017) findings include the theme of role models as important to persistence in Black males. Specifically, participants reported mothers and church pastors as the most common role models. There was no clarification of the sex of the pastors, but it was implied that they were male. The other role models that the participants in the study mentioned were Dr. Martin Luther King Jr., President Barack Obama, and athletic coaches. This research adds to the persistence literature by outlining a detailed perspective on father figures' roles in the family dynamics of Black male students. Another contribution of this study is the highlighting of the higher numbers of Black males who are raised in single-parent households and their concomitant risks and challenges, both in general and when pursuing higher education. These elements add value to the existing literature in terms of representing participants from these more refined categories.

Tolliver and Miller (2018) further the empirical research in support of the theme of role models with Black males in college. The study aimed to identify resources to improve persistence and retention of Black male students. This phenomenological study utilized purposeful sampling to recruit participants. The 11 participants (eight face-to-face, three by telephone) participated in 60 to 90-minute-long structured interviews. The contrast between Tolliver and Miller (2018) and Orrock and Clark (2018) is the makeup of the participants. These two studies approached Black males at very different stages of life. As mentioned above, Orrock and Clark (2018) interviewed Black male high school students who were exclusively raised by single mothers while Tolliver and Miller (2018) interviewed Black males who held advanced degrees and were 25 years and older.

Data were transcribed and analyzed through bracketing, triangulation, and member checking. Four different themes emerged: (a) mentorship, (b) socialization, (c) on-campus supports, and (d) family expectations. Nearly all participants in Tolliver and Miller's (2018) study mentioned mentorship as a key component to persistence in higher education. Conceptually, the citing of the importance of role models by Orrock and Clark (2018) and Holliday and Strange (2013) could be grouped under the notion of mentorship as posited by Tolliver and Miller (2018). The theme of socialization in the latter focused on students' feelings of exclusion due to the differences in culture between their family and community backgrounds and the college atmosphere. Participants reported the necessity of learning how to navigate between the two cultures. The theme of on-campus supports as a theme coupled with the theme of socialization in that participants reported the need for places like multicultural centers to increase possibilities of meeting students with similar world views and backgrounds (Tolliver & Miller, 2018). Similar to Brooks (2015), Tolliver and Miller (2018) mentioned expectations of family as a source of motivation. What is unique about the Tolliver and Miller (2018) study is the addition of community expectations under the theme of family. According to participants of the Tolliver and Miller (2018) study, community expectations referred mostly to members of communities of lower socioeconomic status who had high regard for participants due to their opportunities to go to college.

The Tolliver and Miller (2018) study adds to the science by adding insight on mentorship and Black males' college persistence. According to a liter ature review conducted by Crisp and Cruz (2009) on mentoring college students, findings indicate that mentoring positively impacts undergraduate student persistence and grade point average. Another contribution that this study offered was the importance of how the community impacts the lives of Black men in college. The concept of community in this context encompasses family, neighborhood, religious affiliations, and community organizations. (Tolliver & Miller, 2018). Another factor that is implied, but not overtly stated by Tolliver and Miller (2018), is the impact of race relations on community.

On-campus racial climates. In discussing worldviews and perspectives, Black males may face challenges due to unwelcoming racial climates (Tinto, 1993). Black males may need to employ various skills to persist through negative stereotypes (Boyd & Mitchell, 2018). With CRT as a lens, Boyd and Mitchell (2018) conducted a qualitative study that looked to highlight how six Black males persisted in higher education. This phenomenological study involved second-year Black male undergraduate students a grade-point average of 2.0 or higher. The study was conducted at a PWI in the Midwest. Email recruitment was used to invite participants. Those who agreed participated in two semi-structured face-to-face interviews on campus. This study utilized naturalistic observation where the researcher studies participants in their natural environment (Boyd & Mitchell, 2018). Interviews were recorded, transcribed, and analyzed using line-by-line coding.

Four themes that emerged from the data were labeled internalization, stereotypes, persistence, and advice. The theme of internalization included emotions feelings, containment (students feeling as if they could not be themselves), and questioning themselves (Boyd & Mitchell, 2018). The theme of stereotypes included prejudices and preconceived notions, threats, microaggressions, and the normalization of stereotypes about Black males. The theme of persistence included confronting stereotypes, ignoring stereotypes, dispelling stereotypes (e.g., utilizing tactics such as codeswitching, overcompensating, or using stereotypes as motivation for success), and alleviating pressure (e.g., choosing culturally competent friend groups to be around). Similar to several studies described above (Holliday & Strange, 2013; Orrock & Clark, 2018; Tolliver & Miller, 2018), the theme of advice included the participants' perspectives on the importance of guidance available for young Black males in higher education (Boyd & Mitchell, 2018).

Throughout these recollections during the interview, participants expressed internalized feelings of anger and frustration to the point of questioning themselves (Boyd & Mitchell, 2018). Participants reported frustration and fatigue from internalizing anger caused by experiences of being stereotyped. Some participants passionately discussed confronting stereotypes and being put in positions to have to defend themselves against racial ignorance. They also reported that their White peers had various assumptions about them as Black males, some of which included believing that they (the participants) knew where to find drugs, that they came from impoverished areas, or that they had great athletic ability (Boyd & Mitchell, 2018). In contrast to studies such as Brooks (2015) and Strayhorn et al. (2017), participants in the Boyd and Mitchell (2018) study used the teaching opportunities and negative treatment from others as motivation to persist, rather than their own family support. Some participants in the Boyd and Michell (2018) study took the opposite approach and practiced ignoring stereotypes. Other participants in the study dispelled stereotypes by utilizing code switching (Gumperz, 1977) to change their language to match those around them in attempt to avoid being mistreated.

Work from Boyd and Mitchell (2018) adds to the science by adding firsthand insight into Black males' experiences of stereotyping in higher education settings.According to Kleider-Offutt, Bond, and Hegerty (2017), as they pertain to Black males, "Afrocentric features such as wide noses and full lips are more often associated with negative stereotypes, such as violence and criminality" (p. 31). Additionally, Boyd and Mitchell (2018), like Tolliver and Miller (2018), discuss the impact of race relations in (college) community settings.

Community expectations. Tying together themes of expectations, community, and early exposure to higher education is the work by Brooms and Davis (2017). This qualitative study involved 59 participants from three different institutions in discovering factors that inspired them to pursue higher education (Brooms & Davis, 2017). The community cultural wealth model (Yosso, 2005) was used as a theoretical framework. This phenomenological study focused on Black males who ranged between 19 and 35 years old and had completed 12 credit hours at three PWIs. Similar to Anumba (2015), convenience and purposive sampling was used (Moustakas, 1994). The recruitment methods in Broom and Davis (2017) were distinctive in that the authors used their preexisting professional relationships with faculty members at two of the three institutions (26 participants and 19 participants, respectively) and used pre-existing personal relationships at the third institution

(14 participants) to gather eligible interviewees (Brooms & Davis, 2017).

Data were analyzed using semi-structured, in-depth interviews that lasted between 45 and 150 minutes. Like Schafer et al. (2013), follow-up surveys were used in the Brooms and Davis (2017) study. Recordings were transcribed and coded to discover themes. The items that emerged from the authors' findings regarding the motivation for Black males to pursue higher education were (a) early exposure during the K-12 years, similar to previous studies (Anumba, 2015; Schafer et al., 2013), (b) expectations from family, similar to previous studies (Brooks, 2015; Orrock & Clark, 2018; Tolliver & Miller, 2018), and (c) personal goals, similar to Anumba (2015). Although Brooms and Davis (2017) found items related to the studies above, a distinction from the rest is the discovery of media influence as a factor. Brooms and Davis (2017) highlight several participants who were inspired to attend college based on their experiences growing up watching shows such as "The Cosby Show" and "A Different World." As a counterpoint to Allen's work on stereotyping in the media, this was mentioned in the context of influence and fondness for the role-model aspects of strong, Black male characters. The following section will examine the literature on Black males in college within the academic domain (Wood & Harris, 2012; Harris & Wood, 2016).

The academic domain. The academic domain includes variables such as student-faculty interactions, utilization of academic services, student study habits (Wood & Harris, 2012; Mason, 1998). Academic services are especially helpful to minority students, as many may come from weaker school systems, owing to the history of underfunding described in Chapter 1. Mangan (2014) reports that minority students often enter college with an academic skillset that is not very strong, stating, "The issue is not that these students are not capable of doing college-level work, it is that too many of them have not, for a myriad of reasons, had the kinds of educational experiences that would effectively maximize those capabilities" (p. 2).

Academic support in college. As stated above, studies such as Anumba (2015) and Strayhorn et al. (2017) presented data that support academic support as a meaningful factor for Black males in higher education. Wood (2014) also examined the importance of academic support. While Anumba (2015) and Strayhorn et al. (2017) looked into overall variables for Black male student persistence in higher education (e.g., social support, community presence, academic support), Wood (2014) focused solely on academic support (e.g., academic program, grade point average, working relationships with faculty). Wood's (2014) study examined the impact of the academic variables on Black male student persistence. In addition to the primary focus on academic variables,

Wood (2014) took the participant sample from Black males who were enrolled in community colleges. This in contrast with the studies of Anumba (2015), Brooks (2015), and Strayhorn et al. (2017), who conducted research in 4-year institutions in different settings (rural and urban) and identification (HBCUs and PWIs).

Wood's (2014) longitudinal study gathered data from a national study administered by the NCES called the Beginning Postsecondary Students Longitudinal Study (BPS). The BPS surveys beginning students at three separate time frames. First, at the end of year one, participants engage by phone or internet to complete a self-administered interview. Second, 3 years after beginning postsecondary education, participants participated in phone interviews. Lastly, 6 years after beginning in postsecondary education, in-person interviews were conducted with willing participants.
Logistic regression was used to analyze approximately 6,350 cases.

Wood's (2014) study suggests students are more likely to persist if they met with faculty, were offered the option to take an incomplete, or withdrew from or repeated a course. This study adds to the science by adding a quantitative assessment to the topic of Black male students' experience related to college persistence. The study also used nationwide data similar to Wood and Williams (2013).

The Wood (2014) study utilized data from the NCES while the Wood and Williams (2013) study utilized data from the Educational Longitudinal Study, a nationwide tracking study that collects information on transitions between high school, college, and the workforce.

Before Wood (2014), Wood and Williams's (2013) study concluded that variables such as extracurricular activities, relationships with faculty, study habits, employment, and support systems were the predictors to retention in Black males in community colleges. This longitudinal study examined survey data that were collected in three segments from 2002 (sophomore year in high school), 2004 (senior year in high school), and 2006 (college, or other transitions). This approach to data collection was like Wood (2014) in that it included a 3-step model to collect previous data. However, Wood and Williams (2013) collected data that began with high school students, while the data from Wood (2014) were all form postsecondary students. Wood and Williams (2013) delimited the data and focused on Black males working from a sample of 39,737 students.

Variables were categorized into four groups (environmental, social, academic, and background). Environmental variables included what was referred to as "environmental pull," which referred to obligations like work, financial challenges, or family responsibilities that "pull" them away from their goal of completing college. Social variables included students' participation in activities such as athletics and student organizations. Academic variables include study habits and interacting with faculty. Background variables include the students' educational goals and the level of education of their parents (Wood & Williams, 2013). Perceptions such as financial hardships and family responsibilities were hypothesized as factors that negatively impact Black male persistence in higher education.

The Wood and Williams (2013) study, like Wood (2014), contributes a longitudinal dataset and analysis to the literature on the persistence of Black men in college settings with Wood and Williams' (2013) study focusing on community college settings. They also corroborated findings from previous retention studies, such as Mason (1998).

Academic support before college. A study that offers additional support to the value of academic variables in Black male persistence is a phenomenological study by Holliday and Strange (2013). This study aimed to identify reasons Black males attend college with the goal of increasing their enrollment. Although this study focused on enrollment, support from studies such as Knaggs et al. (2015) found that attitudes about college impact enrollment, attendance, and persistence outcomes. Holliday and Strange (2013) utilized recorded face-to-face interviews of 18 Black males enrolled at a university in Chicago, Illinois. In this phenomenological study, participants were undergraduate students who were within their first 2 years of college and at least 19 years old. Participants were identified from a database at the institution and responded to open-interview survey questions.

In contrast to Wood and Williams (2013) and Wood (2014), findings in Holliday and Strange (2013) highlight academic support during K-12 years as a catalyst to attending college as opposed to just receiving academic support when in college. Although Holliday and Strange (2013) focus on support before college, the data are relevant to this review as precollegiate, or background variables, are widely agreed to be critical factors in many retention models (Bean, 1980, 1982; Bean & Metzner, 1985; Harris & Wood, 2013, 2016; Mason, 1998; Spady, 1980; Tinto, 1975, 1993). Harris and Wood (2013) defined precollegiate variables as factors and experiences that take place before college that influence student success. Some of the variables identified are students' goals, background, and biases that shape perceptions of Black males (Wood & Harris, 2012).

Academic guidance. Holliday and Strange (2013) articulate an argument that Black males have more success in higher education when guided through test-taking skills, application processes, financial aid, and college tours during high school. What is unique to Holliday and Strange (2017) is the mention of participants' choice of academic programs. Like Anumba (2015) and Strayhorn et al. (2017), support systems are mentioned in Holliday and Strange (2017) as a theme in the findings. However, the identification of religion and the church being a significant factor in Black male persistence in higher education was specific to Holliday and Strange (2017).

In speaking about academic support, studies such as Holliday and Strange (2017) and Strayhorn et al. (2017) mention Black male students needing guidance in terms of receiving academic support. Receiving academic support is, in part, having the guidance to know what resources may be available (Holliday & Strange, 2017). More empirical studies that address the background and family dynamics of Black male college students who receive academic support will be discussed further. Whether access to tutoring, peer study groups, or academic help programs, both qualitative and quantitative studies show a theme of the importance of academic support to ensuring Black males persist in higher education. This is also consistent with Harris and Wood (2013) as one of the major findings in the literature reviewed here.

The institutional domain. According to Wood and Harris (2012) and Harris and Wood (2016), the institutional domain includes things such as campus resources, policies, and programs that make up the campus climate. Although similar to the academic domain, the difference in the institutional domain is responsibility. For example, the academic domain focuses more on the student's responsibility to utilize the services, attend classes, interact with faculty, maintain good study habits, and so on. The institutional domain refers to the college's responsibility to offer adequate services to assist with student success. The institutional domain speaks to the overall campus climate and campus resources (programs, policies, and practices) (Wood & Harris, 2012). Literature that addresses the institutional domain (Wood & Harris, 2012; Harris & Wood, 2016) is categorized under campus climate.

Campus climate as a factor for persistence. A study by Cabrera, Nora, Terenzini, Pascarella, and Hagedorn (1999) highlights the impact of campus climate as a factor for persistence. Caberera et al. (1999) investigate racial climates and how Black students' interaction with a hostile environment significantly reduced commitment. This study utilized a quantitative approach to examine how prejudice and discrimination impact Black and White students on college campuses.

Data from incoming first-year students at 18 4-year institutions were utilized in the study.

The IPEDS database was used to invited 1,454 students (315 Black) from 4-year institutions as participants. The study was based on a couple of models. The first was the student adjustment model by Nora and Cabrera (1996). Similar to Tinto (1975, 1993), Nora and Cabrera (1996) posit that students' involvement in academic and social systems are more committed to completing college. The second model used by Cabrera et al. (1999) is Cabrera and Nora's (1994) model perceptions of prejudice and discrimination. This model consists of four measures about students' experience which include: (a) heard negative words about minorities students during classes, (b) believed minority students faced prejudice, (c) witnessed discriminatory actions toward minority students, and(d) felt that instructors treated all students the same regardless of race and ethnicity (Cabrera & Nora, 1994).

Data were analyzed using PRELIS 2.02 software (Joreskog & Sorbom, 1988, 1993) and found that there were no differences in perceptions of prejudice and discrimination between Black and White students. Other findings were that Black students were less likely to report positive experiences with peers than White students. Findings also report that both Black and White students were content with faculty members, and received the same amount of family support (Cabrera et al., 1999).

Student involvement on campus. In contrast with Caberera et al. (1999) is the study by Bush and Bush (2010), who researched Black male achievement incommunity colleges in California. This mixed-method study tested effects institutional factors on Black male perceptions of college experiences. Bush and Bush (2010) identified institutional variables as (a) students' formal and informal interactions with faculty members; (b) student involvement campus clubs, organizations, extracurri- cular activities; (c) campus climate (engagement); and (d) interactions with peers.

Survey data for this study were collected over 6 years using Inland Community College District's student survey data (Bush & Bush, 2010). Students completed admission applications that contained questions about their background and goals. A sample of 1,600 students was stratified by ethnicity and gender. Students then participated in interviews to explore their reasons for leaving or persisting. Data also included a focus group comprised of six Black males between the ages of 18 and 25.

Findings from the study suggest that Black males are more dissatisfied with their campus climate than other ethnic groups (Bush & Bush, 2010). The study elaborated by stating that Black males are less likely to meet with faculty, advisors, or counselors outside of the classroom. A more in-depth study on campus climates and Black students comes from Mwangi, Thelamour, and Ezeofor (2018). This study focused on both Black males and Black females. The themes that emerged were perceptions of Blackness, campus climate, engaging in movements on campus, and the impact of racial climates on future planning (Mwangi et al., 2018).

Like Bush and Bush (2010), Mwangi et al. (2018) used a mixed-methods approach to study Black American and Black immigrant college students and how they navigated campus racial climates. A final sample of 351 participants who chose to complete the survey, and 24 who opted to participate in Zoom interviews (Mwangi et al., 2018

GAPS IN THE LITERATURE AND RECOMMENDATIONS

Several gaps emerged in the literature on Black male persistence in higher educational institutions. Only three studies focused specifically on Black males in community colleges. More recent empirical studies are needed to address inequities involving the rate at which Black males complete college degrees, especially at the community college level (Harris & Wood, 2013; Mason, 1994, 1998; Wood & Turner, 2011). A lack of community college studies is one of the original concerns of Mason (1998), who focused on the Chicago,

Illinois area. Community colleges provide access to postsecondary education for many Black students (Wood, 2011; Wood & Turner, 2011). Based on the sparse number of empirical studies on Black male persistence in community colleges and the disparity in college completion rates of Black males, there is a need for further research that looks to find possible ways to improve academic success rates for Black males (Harris & Wood, 2013; Mason, 1994, 1998; Wood & Turner, 2011) as well as to discover why this disparity exists and persists.

Another literature gap is the lack of data collection from auxiliary staff, faculty, and administrators. Doing so could provide insight into the persistence of Black males in higher education. Also, many researchers report findings on Black males in higher education in southern and western regions of the United States. However, there have been no studies, to date, conducted in the New York State area.

Another gap that emerged in this literature review is that fathers are not mentioned, other than discussion of their absence from the lives of many Black male students. Furthermore, there are no inquiries nor mention of any of the participants being fathers themselves. Although many of the empirical studies reviewed highlight the importance of family relationships, most of the discussion is about the role of the mothers in the lives of the participants.

SUMMARY

According to the McFarland et al. (2018), Black males have the lowest percentage of earned/completed secondary degrees in comparison to their White, Latinx, and Asian counterparts, despite an increase in postsecondary degrees earned nationwide. Between the most recently recorded years of 2013 to 2016, Black males earned associate degrees in the range of 15.5% to 16.9% of such degrees granted (NCES, n.d.). Studies demonstrate that the lack of earned college degrees often correlates with lower socioeconomic status, which in turn has links to health concerns, unemployment, poverty, and incarceration rates (Mirowsky & Ross, 2003; Palmer et al., 2014; Vuolo et al., 2016).

According to the National Urban League (2014), Black undergraduate students are more likely to leave school without completing a degree within 6 years. Despite the numerous studies on Black males in higher education, less attention has been directed toward Black males in community college settings, specifically, which is arguably a significant oversight, considering the importance these institutions have in the lives of Black men, among others, striving for better life outcomes. For Black males to increase their overall college success rates, there needs to be more focus on retention, specifically for Black males in community college settings (Mason, 1998).

The literature review by Harris and Wood (2013) found that academic, environmental, noncognitive, institutional, and social domains are the major factors in Black male persistence in community colleges. This review found that self-efficacy, social support, academic support, male role model influence, and campus climate are significant factors as they pertain to persistence in Black males in community colleges. The variables found in this review fit in four of the five domains of Wood and Harris (2012) and Harris and Wood (2016). Although social factors are identified in the literature review for this dissertation study, they did not fit neatly into the social domain as presented by Wood and Harris (2012) and Harris and Wood (2016) and are thus considered redundant.

Empirical studies suggest that the social support factor for persistence in Black males includes family, friends, and encouragement from neighborhood communities (which also fall under the environmental domain). The literature states that these elements are needed to serve as motivating factors for pushing through adversity that Black males may face during the education process. The literature also suggests that academically, Black males will benefit from precollegiate exposure to college and easily accessible academic support (e.g., tutoring, advisement, counseling) when in college in order to persist through to graduation. These are necessary to compensate for the possible deficits arising from a lack of academic preparation or current academic struggles. An integral aspect of persistence for Black males in community college settings that emerges from the literature is the importance of male role models. The literature states that male role models and mentors are either greatly appreciated or severely missed. Socioeconomic factors also emerge as a theme in this literature review. For Black males to persist in community college settings, financial struggles must be manageable. Wood and Harris (2013) find that financial matters impacted college choice in Black male students. Empirical studies also support the premise that social class, parents' education, and cost play a role in persistence in higher education (Harris & Wood, 2013).

The literature review yields several insights into Black male student persistence in higher education, but few that focus specifically on Black males in community college settings. Out of these few results that do, even fewer are from the last 5 years. Literature that addresses the Black male student persistence in community colleges is minimal compared to those of traditional students at 4-year institutions.

Chapter 2 presents a literature review of the empirical research studies on Black male persistence in higher education. Differences and similarities in the studies' purposes, methodologies, strategies of inquiry, data collection methods, findings, and arguments were compared. This literature review highlights how these studies connect to corroborate or refute the data and their interpretations. Also reviewed were studies on the persistence of Black males in higher education settings. Furthermore, gaps in the research were identified while also providing possible opportunities for further research. Chapter 3 presents the methodology for the study.

CHAPTER 3

RESEARCH DESIGN METHODOLOGY

INTRODUCTION

Chapter 2 presented a review of the literature on Black male persistence in higher education. Factors for Black male persistence in college settings were discussed, as well as the social constructs of Black male identity. Research gaps in the existing knowledge related to Black males in higher education were identified. A significant gap emerging from the literature review is the lack of attention to fathers, other than stating that many are absent from the lives of many Black male students and the consequences and implications of this absence. Furthermore, no inquiry pursued questions about the fatherhood of participants in studies, nor discussed the role of fatherhood in education persistence for any of the participants. Other gaps in the literature include the low number of qualitative studies conducted to explore Black male persistence in higher educational institutions and few studies that focus specifically on Black males in community college settings. This dissertation focused on the intersection of Black fatherhood and Black male persistence in community colleges. This study endeavors to carve out a novel area of interest while contributing to the general body of literature on Black males in higher education.

RESEARCH QUESTIONS AND PURPOSE OF THE STUDY

The purpose of this study was to examine how Black fathers perceive fatherhood (their own and their fathers') and how it impacts persistence in community college. Specifically, the following research questions guided the study:

1. How do Black male college students experience fatherhood (from a son's perspective) facilitating, or impeding, community college completion?

2. How do Black male college students experience their fatherhood facilitating, or impeding, community college completion?

3. In the experience of Black male college students, how do community colleges support Black students who are fathers?

DESIGN

This study investigated Black student-fathers' perceptions of navigating community college using a transcendental phenomenological approach (Moustakas, 1994). Black males are historically and continually underrepresented in education, media, and politics. This results in other people defining and speaking for their experiences rather than themselves. Lived experience refers not just to experience, but to the notion of embodied experience. It is important for marginalized populations to articulate their own embodied experience because without their voices, their lived experience may be misconstrued, misrepresented, and even be coopted and used to serve ends, political and otherwise, not their own.

The lived experience is especially important for Black men in general, but also for Black fathers and Black men in academic environments. Each of these forms of embodiment—as a father, son, man, student—carry their own personal meanings. For Black men who embody these roles, there is a politicization of their experiences and existence that complicates their experience. The intersections of being Black, a father, and pursuing higher education creates a specific type of embodied experience that carries its own implications and meanings that ideally are defined and expressed by those who live this particular experience.

TRANSCENDENTAL PHENOMENOLOGY

Transcendental phenomenology explores phenomena as they appear in our experiences (Moustakas, 1994). This methodological design was the best fit for this study as the goal was to discover the essence of the phenomena of this specific population. The process is broken down into four parts: (a) epoche, (b) phenomenological reduction, (c) imaginative variation, and (d) synthesis (Moustakas, 1994). Epoche (bracketing) is when the researcher removes biases and preconceived thoughts. Phenomenological reduction (horizontalization) is when the researcher collects data on the participants' experiences and gives equal value to the textural descriptions. During imaginative variation, the researcher examines and interprets the experiences. Synthesis is combining the textural and structural descriptions to uncover the essence of the phenomenon (Moustakas, 1994).

The transcendental phenomenological design for this study prioritizes giving voice to Black student-fathers and looking at their experience from as many angles as possible. According to Moustakas (1994), transcendental phenomenology was developed by Husserl and considered to be a rational path that describes how participants experience phenomena in the world. Transcendental phenomenology is useful for describing phenomena through participants' experiences, perceptions, and voices. The resulting rich dataset provides more than enough material for analysis.

Moustakas (1994) contends that transcendental phenomenology focuses on rich, textural descriptions as the essence of a study. Since participants' lived experiences were the focal point of the study, they were given the opportunity to express themselves freely. The phenomenon under observation in the study was how the fatherhood/son experience impacted persistence in Black community college students.

PROCEDURE

The study received IRB approval from St. John Fisher College. Participants were recruited through snowball sampling. Flyers were distributed through social media and digital bulletin boards through emails at several community colleges in New York State. The researcher also contacted the deans of students and administrators at several community colleges and described the study. Those who agreed to assist the researcher distributed the digital flyers, which included a description of the study and researcher contact information, via student emails on the researcher's behalf. Potential participants were requested to respond to the researcher's St. John Fisher email listed on the flyer to set up an appointment for a Zoom interview. Zoom interviews were used, instead of the original plan for face-to-face interviews, for safety reasons due to the COVID-19 pandemic.

The researcher received consent from the participants. Once the participant gave permission to record, the researcher began recording the interview and read the consent form. Participants then gave their verbal recorded consent. Interviews lasted between 55 minutes to 1 hour and 30 minutes.

The set of questions and directives provided the participants with opportunities to truly tell their story. The informal structure and open-ended nature of the discussion provided a comfortable atmosphere. The conversation came across as engaged and interested but not invasive. Even though the participants were encouraged to share openly, they were requested to choose pseudonyms. Pseudonyms for each participant were used to label the recordings. All audio recordings of interviews were transcribed through Rev.com for data analysis. Once interviews were transcribed, recordings (audio and video) were deleted.

PARTICIPANTS

The population for this study was Black male, actively enrolled, community college students with biological children. This population of students was selected through purposeful sampling. Purposeful sampling (Creswell & Poth, 2018) was used to identify six participants. Bungay, Oliffe, and Atchinson (2016) described purposeful sampling as a strategic selection of rich cases for data collection.

Participant descriptions. Table 3.1 provides a short description of the six participants.

Setting. As stated in Chapter 1, the importance of community colleges is recognized for their accessibility for so many students Melguizo, Kienzl, and Kosiewicz (2013), and O'Banion (2013). Community colleges offer convenience in things such as location, course offerings, and less stringent acceptance requirements. This study included interviews with six Black student-fathers from three different community colleges in New York State. The community college enrollments were between 7% and 16% Black students.

Table 3.1

Participant Demographics

Name	Age	Degree Program	G.P.A.	Children	Participation in Campus Activities
Zion	56	Criminal Justice	3.0	Daughter (34) Son (33)	N/A
Isaiah	31	Business Administration	Unsure	Son (9) Son (5) Daughter (1)	African Students Club
Joshua	33	Communications	3.7	Daughter (14)	National Society of Leadership and Success
Zachariah	47	Digital Media	3.7	Son (29) Daughter (21) Son (16)	-Phi Theta Kappa Honors Society -School newspaper (writer) -Media Club

| Thaddeus | 43 | Human Services | 3.8 | Daughter (22) Daughter (20) Son – (deceased at 14, would have been 18) | -Phi Theta Kappa Honors Society -Black Student Union |
| Ishmael | 36 | Health Sciences | 3.5 | Son (16) Daughter (14) Son (6) | -Tutoring -Student Fun Night |

Instruments. There were two instruments utilized in this study. The first instrument was the demographics form (Appendix A). The demographic data collected from participants before the interviews were as follows: (a) Name, (b) Age, (c) What is your enrollment status? (d) Do you take classes primarily online, or primarily on campus? (e) What degree or certificate program are you in? (f) What is your GPA? (g) What is your primary campus? (h) When did you begin at the college? (i) How are you paying for classes? (j) Have you participated in any campus activities (athletics, student government)? (k) If yes, which ones? (l) What is your employment status? (m) What is your relationship status? and (n) Do you live with your child(ren)? The questions were selected to contextualize the rich descriptive data to be gathered.

The second instrument the study employed was the semi-structured interview. The questions and directives were as follows: (a) Please share your journey into fatherhood. (b) What was it like growing up as a son? (c) Did your parents go to college? (d) Describe your academic journey and how you arrived at the College. (e) How has being a Black male and a father impacted your experience at the College? (f) What does your college do to assist you as a Black male and as a father? and (g) What can your college do to increase your success as a Black male, and as a father?

ANALYSIS

Data were analyzed through Moustakas' (1994) transcendental phenomenological methods of epoche, horizontalization, clustering into themes, textural descriptions, structural descriptions, and textural-structural synthesis.

Epoche. During the epoche the researcher engaged in reflexivity. As a Black male who was also a father while attending community college, the researcher recognized the possibility of preconceptions. Through reflexivity, the researcher looked to explore his own responses to participant data and experiences. The researcher utilized a journal before, during, and after data collection in order to keep a record of personal thoughts and feelings regarding Black males, fatherhood, and educational attainment. According to Teh and Lek (2018), reflexivity can assist in the assurance of quality and trustworthiness in qualitative research. Reflective field notes and journal entries were used to document the researcher's interpretations and personal thoughts that could impact the research.

Phenomenological reduction. Phenomenological reduction is the process by which the researcher breaks down the understanding of concepts from a worldly view and focuses on the participant's experience of a phenomenon (Moustakas, 1994). This process was essential due to the individuality of each participant's experiences of the phenomenon—fatherhood as a Black community college student—under investigation. The unique dual perspective of this study from a father's point of view, as well as a son's point of view, was highlighted.

Horizontalization. According to Moustakas (1994), horizontalization is another mode of phenomenological reduction. Horizontalization is the listing of relevant quotes from the data and giving them equal value (Padilla-Diaz, 2015). Most importantly, the data are viewed without the researcher's interpretations.

To effectively engage in horizontalization, all interview data were transcribed through Rev.com and reviewed by the researcher. All data were collected firsthand by the researcher to ensure authenticity. Initially, all statements had equal value, meaning that no statement is considered more important than another (Moustakas, 1994). Horizontalization took place through reading the transcribed interviews several times and coding them based on significant statements. Significant statements that emerged from the data were assigned as themes, such as "lack of support." Overlapping statements between the participants were eliminated (Moustakas, 1994).

Cluster into themes. According to Moustakas (1994), a theme is a word or phrase that is used frequently during the data collection process. The purpose of themes is to allow the data to yield similarities or corroborations among the participants without bias from the researcher. Participant responses were categorized according to the most frequently used words and concepts. The objective was for the themes to contribute to the rich, descriptive analysis of the phenomenon.

Textural descriptions. Textural descriptions refer to the description of what is expressed by the participants (Padilla-Diaz, 2015). In this study, the participants provided vivid descriptions of their experiences as Black student-fathers in community college settings. Rich descriptions of participants' feelings and emotions about their experiences embodying this phenomenon were documented by the researcher (Moustakas, 1994). Participant quotes were used to highlight and understand the experiences. "Perceptions bring textural descriptions to life, in explicating the 'what' of our experience" (Moustakas, 1994, p. 81). Finding the "what" of the experience allowed for a complete and accurate representation of the group (Moustakas, 1994; Padilla-Diaz, 2015).

Structural descriptions. As stated above, textural descriptions are designed to represent the "what" of the phenomenon. Structural descriptions refer to the interpretation or "how" a given phenomenon is expressed by the participants (Moustakas, 1994; Padilla-Diaz, 2015). Essentially, the structure of each participant's experience is fused into a main description. Combined with the textural descriptions, structural descriptions are utilized for the purposes of synthesis.

Textural-structural synthesis. Moustakas (1994) describes textural-structural synthesis as the final step designed to synthesize the "what" and the "how" of the experience to extract the overall essence (Moustakas, 1994). The textural-structural synthesis in study utilized the data interviews, demographic forms, and the researcher's reflective notes. The textural-structural synthesis for this study took Black student-fathers' experiences in community college settings, and created a full, comprehensive description.

CONCLUSION

This chapter reviewed the research methods used in the study. Transcendental phenomenology was used to describe and analyze the lived experiences of this specific population. The transcendental phenomenological design promoted the examination of the interactions between measurable outcomes with immeasurable qualities, like perceptions and experiences (Moustakas, 1994). The study focused primarily on Black student-fathers' in community colleges. Chapters 4 and 5 present the findings and conclusions of this study.

CHAPTER 4

RESULTS

INTRODUCTION

The purpose of Chapter 4 is to highlight the experiences of Black student-fathers in community colleges and gain a better understanding of any impact that fatherhood has, or has had, on their persistence in completing degrees. These experiences will be expressed through the voices of the participants. Table 4.1 presents an overview of the research questions, themes, and subthemes.

Table 4.1

Research Questions, Themes, and Subthemes

Research Questions	Themes	Subthemes
How do Black male college students experience fatherhood (from a son's perspective) facilitating or impeding community college completion?	Parenting Matters	Healthy Parenting Unhealthy Parenting
How do Black male college students experience their fatherhood (from a father's perspective) facilitating or impeding community college completion?	Impenetrable Lifelong Connections Resilience and Progress Desire to be Living Proof	
In the experience of Black male college students, how do community colleges support Black students who are fathers?	Typical Unnecessary Obstacles True Acknowledgement And Acceptance	Lack of Support Racism

Table 4.2 presents an overview of the overarching research question and the findings based on the themes and subthemes.

Although the participants responded to the same interview questions, certain characteristics stood out in each one. Zion's narrative had a heavy focus on overcoming

Table 4.2

Overarching Research Question and Findings

Overarching Research Question	Findings Based on Themes and Subthemes
How do Black males perceive fatherhood (their own and their father's), and how it impacts their persistence in community college?	Parenting acts as a catalyst to community college completion for Black student-fathers Children are at the center of persistence for Black student-fathers Support Systems are lacking for Black student-fathers

addiction. Isaiah's responses focused on cross-cultural experiences between Africa and America. Joshua's stories focused on the strained relationship with his father, and his dedication to his only daughter. Zachariah's narrative focused on his journey from adoption to fatherhood. Thaddeus' stories focused on the painful loss of his youngest son to suicide. Ishmael's responses focused on the absence of a father figure to guide him through difficult times.

THEMES

This section highlights the themes and subthemes that emerged from the data. Answers to the three research questions were provided through participant quotes.

Research Question 1. Research Question 1 (RQ1) examined how Black male community college students experience fatherhood (from a son's perspective) facilitating or impeding community college completion. Participants reported parenting matters with subthemes of (a) healthy parenting and (b) unhealthy parenting. Table 4.3 presents the theme, two subthemes, and four key concepts that emerged from RQ1.

Table 4.3

RQ1 – Theme, Subthemes, and Key Concepts

Theme	Key Concepts	Subthemes
	Financial Support Discipline Responsibility Effort	Healthy Parenting

"Parenting Matters"	Lack of Emotional Support Father Not Present Parent's Strained Relationship	Unhealthy parenting

The parenting matters theme emerged through participants' explanations of how the parenting they received mattered in establishing, developing, and nurturing relationships with their children. Parenting that the participants received also facilitated their community college completion. When asked the question, "Can you talk about an experience you had as a son that helped to shape your approach as a father?" all six participants made statements about their father's relationship with their mothers, and how the parenting dynamic took place. The status of the relationship between the father and mother dictated the relationship between the father and son. The two participants in this study with no father figure report that the relationship between the fathers and mothers was strained or nonexistent. The participants with better experiences with their fathers reported that it was based on the cohesive family unit that began with the father and mother's strong relationship. The duality of the impact of parenting manifested into subthemes of healthy and unhealthy parenting.

Healthy parenting. This subtheme emerged from participants mentioning being brought up in family circumstances where their fathers emphasized discipline, financial support, responsibility, and putting forth their best effort regardless of circumstance. Four of the six participants reported that there was a teamwork or partnership effect within the family structure with the father as the head. These parenting measures helped the participants become the fathers they are today, as well as facilitated community college completion. In one participant's case, he also had an uncle as part of the disciplinary aspect of the family. Zachariah is between the ages of 45-50. He became a father 2 weeks before his 18th birthday. Zachariah is a full-time student majoring in communications with a grade point average of 3.7. When asked to talk about an experience he had as a son that helped to shape his approach as a father, Zachariah responded with the following:

> I got my parenting style from my mother, who loved me too much, my father, who was too harsh of a disciplinarian, and then my uncle who would tell you why he was disciplining you and would talk to you. So, I adopted all three of those styles to become a father Shaolin master.

Zachariah used the term "Shaolin master" as a metaphor to accentuate his feelings of well-rounded expertise in fatherhood. Shaolin master is in reference to the popular notion of Chinese monks who specialize in martial arts and spiritual discipline.

When telling his story about an experience as a son that helped to shape his approach as a father, Thaddeus said that his father worked hard every day and made sure that his children witnessed him giving money to their mother each week to pay the bills. Thaddeus is 43 years old and became a father at 19 years old. Thaddeus is a full-time student majoring in Human Services with a 3.8 grade point average. He went on to state that during that weekly routine, the children would also experience their father giving them their earned allowance. Thaddeus stated that "taking care of your own" was one of the main lessons that he received from his father. He explained that watching his father consistently provide for the family, no matter his mood or the circumstances, taught him to always take care of his family responsibilities.

While reflecting on the same question of how experience as a son shaped fatherhood, Isaiah added a different cultural perspective. Isaiah is between the ages of 30-35. He became a father at 23 years old. Isaiah is enrolled as a full-time student majoring in business and was unsure about his grade point average. He described growing up in West Africa where his father did his best to make sure that he and his siblings had a better life than many others in their community. Like Thaddeus, he talked about his father being a leader and setting a good example for his children. Isaiah repeated a phrase from his native country in Africa. He stated, "We say, such father, such son." Isaiah continued, "Yes, in French, it means that a child, a baby, or a son is the product of his father." Isaiah agreed that his solid foundation and experience with a good father was the catalyst to becoming a responsible father himself. As Isaiah talked about college persistence, he repeated the sentiment "Such father, such son," about setting an example for his own children by pursuing education.

Four of the six participants mentioned their father's financial support of the family as a fundamental characteristic of healthy parenting. This was the case even when the father's financial contribution was not that much. In these instances, participants spoke about how the significance of their father's efforts made the dollar amounts seem less important. When reflecting on the scarcity of resources growing up, recognition of the father's hard work and resilience was highlighted. Zion was between the ages of 55 and 60 years old and became a father when he was 23 years old. Zion is a full-time student majoring in criminal justice with a 3.0 grade point average. When speaking about his father's hard work, he shared:

> One of the main things is growing up not having enough. You know from Arkansas; my dad was a carpenter. He did carpenter work, but he wasn't a licensed carpenter. He was a licensed plumber but there wasn't a lot of plumbing opportunities for him.

Zion mentioned that it was often a struggle for this father to support everyone in his large family. In addition to appreciating his father's efforts, the experience of not having a lot as one of 10 children served as a motivator for his own experience of fatherhood. When expounding on the connection between his experience as a son and his direction as a father, Zion explained:

There wasn't a lot of financial resources coming into the house, but they did the best they could, though, because there were 10 of us. And so, the experience was, 'cause we all would say when we had kids, we were gonna make sure that they had everything that they needed. And so therefore, I was determined . . . take care of them and be the best father I could be.

Despite having healthy parenting and becoming better fathers to their children, some participants reported having made bad choices as fathers, which negatively impacted their lives. The experience of being a son to becoming a father was complicated for Thaddeus. Since his father demonstrated such a healthy parenting dynamic that included an intact marriage, Thaddeus experienced feelings of inadequacy due to his inability to replicate the same circumstances. Thaddeus felt that his inability to maintain his healthy parenting due to divorce led to a tragedy involving his son. His volatile marriage ending and resulted in him moving back to his home state to where he had support and could get himself back together emotionally and financially. However, he later made a choice to make it right for his children. When describing his struggles during that time, Thaddeus expressed:

> So, I felt like I let them down, because I couldn't get the marriage to work, even though I feel different now. I think it was a good thing that we didn't stay together. But I felt like a failure because I was raised with both my parents. I felt like a total failure because I'm used to a certain level of stuff. When my son died,

it's a whole different emotion, because he's the one that used to call me all the time. He was the youngest. He was the one that looked like me.

Thaddeus felt that his inability to maintain the family unit the way his father did resulted in ineffective co-parenting. This separation caused him to be away from his son when he needed him the most. Thaddeus discussed feeling like things would have been different if he were there with his son. He blamed himself for at least a year and turned to religion to cope with the pain. When discussing his son, Thaddeus recalled:

> When he was 7, he could read any book you put in front of him. They had him in a special gifted and talented school. He had told me that he didn't really want to be in there anymore, but his mama pressured him to stay in there, because of some other stuff. A lot of different things happened I felt wouldn't have happened if I was there. I'm blaming myself. That, if I was there, that wouldn't have happened. If I was there, my baby would still be here. That's why Ihad to give it to God. Because I blamed myself for it, for at least a straight year.

Another example of bad choices some participants made despite having healthy parenting included addiction. Three of the six participants talked about their experiences overcoming addiction. Those three participants all had fathers who exhibited healthy parenting. While Thaddeus became addicted to alcohol after the loss of his son, Zachariah became addicted to crack cocaine. Zachariah explained how the beginning of his addiction to crack was smoking marijuana. He then began to depend on the heavier drugs. According to Zachariah:

> The first time I ever tried weed was when I was 14. It was at a party. It was a little roach. Didn't get high. Several years later after that, I had a friend who was sitting in the park. She had a whole blunt. I smoked a blunt with her. And there the precursor of a crackhead was born.

Zachariah stated that he understood why marijuana is often said to lead to using other drugs from personal experience. He explained:

> Smoking weed and all of that, then I got into the pattern, so being so secluded. I got addicted to crack. Then I realized why they call weed a crossover drug. And the reason is because although it doesn't have the same addictive qualities, but back then it wasn't so much the addiction to the weed. It was the lifestyle, the sneaking around, the spending the money, the isolating yourself, only being around other people who smoked weed. And so those are the things that set you up to become an addict.

Although Zachariah talked about the fast lifestyle, he explained that the influence from a romantic partner led to his addiction. He stated:

> Over the years, what ended up happening is I let a girl move in with me that had drug problems. We went to a weed spot where they sold weed and crack, and I just said, "Hey, give me one. I want to try it."

Thaddeus talked about his addiction taking place after his divorce. He stated:

> After my divorce, I had somewhat of a drinking problem. I left my house, I left everything down there, even though I'm not upset about it because my kids were living there. I bought my house because each one of them had their own bedroom.

Participants discussed how experiencing healthy parenting as sons shaped their experiences as fathers. Four of the six participants mentioned experiencing healthy parenting, which included their fathers having good relationships with their mothers. The participants internalized these experiences and used them as guidelines to establish themselves as fathers, as well as facilitate college completion.

Unhealthy parenting. This subtheme emerged from some of the participants mentioning going through childhood without a father figure to guide them. Others mentioned that despite their father being present, there was no connection or emotional support to nurture them. Although they had connections with and received emotional support from their mothers, they still felt a void. The unhealthy parenting in this study came from participants' expressions of said void as well as feelings of damage caused by neglect or emotional abuse from their fathers.

The theme of healthy parenting highlighted financial support and discipline. The theme of unhealthy parenting prioritized emotional support. Participants who grew up devoid of their father's emotional support made a promise to be better fathers to their children. When asked to speak about an experience he had as a son that helped to shape his approach as a father, Joshua explained learning from the mistakes that his father made by not being very involved with him, and his brother. Joshua is between the ages of 30-35. He became a father at 20 years old. Joshua was enrolled as a full-time student majoring in communications with a 3.7 grade point average. When speaking about his father, Joshua stated, "There was never a time where he really tried to sit down and talk, and get to really know who I am, and what I'm interested in."

Joshua's father was in the home with him until he was 12 years old. Reflecting on his adult relationship with his father, Joshua explained that the lack of relationship is apparent to others, and that is something that he would work to prevent with his own child. According to Joshua:

> Me and my dad, we are identical, I'm a lighter version of him, looks and everything, and he worked at the hospital, so everybody knows him, and people there know me because I worked at Children's Hospital. It was across from each other. But you could see that we're related, but you couldn't tell what the relation was because it was like there was no communication.

This situation reminded Joshua of what he did not want when his daughter became an adult. He said, "It was just like two complete strangers just sitting next to each other." Joshua also spoke about the fact that his father's attention was split due to a secret romantic relationship with another woman. He mentioned, "Pretty much since my brother was born, my dad had an ongoing girlfriend. My brother is 38. So, from my brother being born until this current time right now as we're even talking, they're still together." His father's affair was the reason why he ultimately left home when Joshua was 12-years old. Joshua explained that although his mother knew many years earlier, he did not find out about his father's other relationship until he was an adult.

Participants who experienced healthy parenting from their fathers learned how to be better fathers based on that positive example. Conversely, participants who experienced unhealthy parenting from their fathers learned how to be fathers from a negative or inconsistent example their fathers modeled. While reflecting on the lack of involvement of his father, and the state of the relationship between the two now, Joshua stated, "I just kept reminding myself, this is why I'm so involved in my daughter's life because this right here is what I don't want. I don't want this relationship to be me and my daughter. That's that."

While Joshua's father was around for the first 12 years of his life, Ishmael's father was barely present at all. However, Ishmael explained how his father's absence growing up helped to shape him to be the father he became. Ishmael is between the ages of 35-40. He was 19 years old when he became a father. Ishmael was enrolled as a full-time student majoring in Health Sciences with a 3.5 grade point average. He described how he did not have a father to teach him how to be a father to his son. Ishmael relied on his mother for advice on how to be a father. He expressed being in the same situation as an adult as he was as a child, where he leaned on his mother for his needs. This dynamic was discussed by Ishmael:

> Because I didn't have that figure in life, like that father figure to tell me, "Well, do this with your son" or "Do that for your son." So it was just like pretty much my mom was helping me and I was just winging it from that there.

While Joshua and Ishmael categorized a lack of presence as unhealthy parenting, Isaiah had a different cultural perspective as an immigrant who moved to the United States at 27 years old. He spoke about how he experienced culture shock when he came to the United States due to what he perceived as a high number of blended families. From a cultural standpoint, Isaiah focused on how important role modeling is in parenting. In describing his experience, Isaiah stated, "Sometimes when your father and mother had these habits, you'll be all those habits." For Isaiah, the idea of a father having children with several different women was associated with unhealthy parenting. He said, "If your father married his second wife, it's not hard for you to have a second wife." Since fathers being role models to their sons was so important to Isaiah, he felt that having multiple children with different women was setting a bad example for the children. Isaiah reflected on a conversation he overheard at his job that illustrated this point. He recalled the story:

> It was like 2 weeks ago, one of my co-workers asked another co-worker, "How many kids?" He said, "Four kids." She asked, "How many wives?" He said, "Only one wife." Then the woman said, "Mm, how is that? How can you have four babies with one woman?"

Isaiah mentioned the differences in family structure between his native country and the United States. His feelings were that in the United States, it is not abnormal for a mother to raise kids by herself, or have children with more than one father. Isaiah stated, "Back home, I can say like 80 or 90% of mothers raise their kids with their husbands." Isaiah expressed the likely inevitability of a father with children with different women being unable to maintain a consistent presence in his children's lives. He expressed it this way:

> You're not gonna stay with all those kids in the same house. It means that another husband will be taking care of them. And the husband, the present husband may not be taking total care of those step kids, let me say.

Directly or indirectly experiencing these unhealthy parenting circumstances opened the participants' minds to becoming better parents, and not follow in the footsteps of their fathers, or other fathers that they observed. This is seen where a participant says that getting recognized for his relationship with his daughter made him feel validated as a "real" father. According to Joshua:

> So those moments when I get the recognition from other people, especially from other cultures, other races because of the stigma that is there for Black fathers not being there for their kids. I want to showcase that you can be there. Even if you don't get along or you and the mother are not together anymore, you can still be a vocal point and an important piece because you are an important piece in the raising of your child.

As a counterpoint to these external validations, Isaiah stated, "I'm the role model of my kid, I don't care when anybody says good things or bad things about me, but I know me, I know what I am. I don't think that anybody can define me."

As Ishmael reflected on his father not being there when he needed him, he reported that he made a promise to himself that he would never leave his child behind "no matter what." Ishmael that he could not bear to see his son suffer as he did as a child. Without his father's guidance, Ishmael sought support, validation, and camaraderie from the streets. Gang affiliations and violence provided opportunities to develop and prove his masculinity and manhood. He stated:

I mean, the more bad stuff I went through, it's like the more I just didn't want my son going through it, though. Like if I see my son veering off to something that I did, then I'll just put a hold to that. Like, "Listen, don't even," you know, "It's not even worth it."

As far as facilitating college completion, Ishmael said, "My son is not going to college yet, but I can say that me going to college right now, I can share the experience with him when he goes off."

Data from the first research question shows that all six participants spoke about the importance of parenting and how it is a catalyst to community college completion. All six participants also spoke about the sense of pride they felt for being in their children's lives, making positive changes, or working to achieve goals to be a good example for them. Four of the six participants discussed how experiencing healthy parenting as sons shaped their experiences as fathers. Two of the six participants mentioned experiencing unhealthy parenting as sons shaped their experiences as fathers. Both subthemes of healthy parenting and unhealthy parenting included participants' fathers' relationships with their mothers. The four participants who experienced healthy parenting used the experience to guide them as fathers, as well as facilitate college completion. The participants who experienced unhealthy parenting used the experiences of having uninvolved, or marginally involved, fathers as motivation to be better fathers to their children, as well as facilitate college completion.

Research Question 2. Research Question 2 (RQ2) examined how Black male community college students experience fatherhood (from a father's perspective) facilitating or impeding community college completion. Participants reported (a) impenetrable connections, (b) resilience and progress, and (c) desire to be "living proof." Table 4.4 presents the three themes and nine key concepts that emerged from RQ2.

Table 4.4

RQ2 – Themes and Key Concepts

Theme	Key Concepts
"Impenetrable Lifelong Connections"	Pregnancy/Birth Shared experiences Fear
"Resilience and Progress"	Recovery Depression Suicide Role Modeling
"Desire to be Living Proof"	Decisions Sacrifice

Impenetrable lifelong connections. This theme emerged with participants expressing the deep emotional bonds that they shared with their children. These experiences, beginning during their children's births, shared experiences, and fears of not being good fathers, helped these Black men to strive to become the best fathers they could be. These experiences also facilitated community college completion. All six participants talked about the impact of their children being born. When asked to describe a time when he truly felt like a father, Zion simply stated about his son, "Well, for one thing, I was there." He went on to speak about the disappointment of missing out on the birth of his first child, and how his ability to be there for the birth of his second child was special. Zion said, "I was there when he was born. Now, I have a daughter also, but me and her mother really wasn't gettin' along too good, anyways." Zion recalled being more involved in the process of his son, which resulted in a newfound experience of fatherhood for him even though it was not his first time being a father. Being present for the birth made fatherhood seem more real for him. Zion talked about his emotions during his son's birth. He stated, "Well, it was kind of like, I don't know what, like elation, excitement. I was blown away, but I was looking forward to it. I was really looking forward to it." Not only was he looking forward to the birth of his son, but he also went on leave from the military just to be there.

When thinking about the birth of his daughter, Joshua spoke about going through a lot of emotions. According to Joshua, he was recently engaged in a conversation about the fear he had the day his daughter was born. He stated:

> So, I was kind of like, "How am I going to be able to raise a child?" You know, I didn't have my father, and my brother was like, "We are going to figure this out. We are going to do what we have to do." And he was like, "It's funny, I'm saying we like it's me and you," and he was like, "But you made a vow. You said as you were holding your daughter when you came back, you said, 'I'm never leaving you. I will always be there, and I'll be the best father I can be.'" And he was like, "And to this day you are the best father I've ever known." So, him bringing that back and then me remembering every year on her birthday, I always remember the moment that she was born.

Joshua reflected on the emotions he felt when he first held his daughter. He said, "I held her, it was scary, because it's like, okay, now I have a responsibility, the biggest responsibility a man can have, raising a child." Zachariah spoke about the births of his children by stating, "Yeah, when I was there for two of my kids' births, so I actually video recorded two of them."

Although the births of their children were cited as meaningful for all the participants, Isaiah took his explanation a bit further. He spoke about creating that bond during pregnancy. According to Isaiah:

I have to start with taking care of, first of all, the pregnancy. That's the beginning fatherhood. To have that good child you need to take care of pregnancy. You know? If you don't prepare, you don't take care of the pregnancy, it means that you're not gonna have a baby of your dreams, you know? Yes, I have to take care of that during the 9 months, I think this is the most important thing to do.

In addition to experiencing the births of their children, other defining moments accentuated the theme of impenetrable connections. For example, when intervening in a family dispute, Joshua recalled having a stern conversation with the parties involved. He mentioned protecting his daughter to the point of risking incarceration. Joshua recalled stating to someone, "I'm her protector. If anything happens to her, I'm possibly going to jail, because that's my daughter." One participant reflected on his feelings while witnessing his son exhibiting the same behaviors as he did at a certain age without any coaching. When recalling a situation when he truly felt like a father, Zachariah explained, "When you see that child doing a lot of the same stuff that you did, and you realize that they came from you, it puts a reflection on your life, and that makes you know that you're a father." Zachariah's statement referred directly to the theme of impenetrable connection by describing the transcendent experience and spiritual realization of just how connected he was with his son. Zachariah saw the significance in looking past the genetic sense of him and his son looking alike.

He realized that certain feelings, behaviors, and mannerisms of his son were just like his own even though he did not teach them. The inherent sense of identity truly highlighted their connection.

Thaddeus spoke about the impenetrable connection between him and his youngest son. He mentioned that even though his son was no longer with him physically, his son deserved the credit for Thaddeus's positive changes. Thaddeus stated:

> Like I said, before he died, I was already doing the drinking, and everything else, or whatnot. I never was into too many drugs, but the drinking, it was killing me. So, I feel that he's my hero. Even though I would have him back in a minute.

Participants discussed how experiencing the impenetrable, spiritual connections between themselves and their children shaped their experiences as fathers. All six participants mentioned experiencing this connection since the births of the children. One participant went as far as to say the connection began during the pregnancy. Three of the six participants spoke to the immense power of the connection to their children. One participant expressed the connection to his daughter as being so strong that he would be willing to go to prison if she were harmed. Another participant spoke about the realization of the deep connection through inherent similarities between himself and his son. The third participant communicated still feeling the connection to his son even though he was no longer alive.

Resilience and progress. This theme emerged with participants reflecting on how being a father shaped their lives, and their determination to make better lives for their children. Most of the participants wanted to be a role model to their children in a way that showed that education has no limit, and they can follow in their footsteps. In relation to resilience, two of the six participants talked about how thoughts of their children convinced them not to move forward with committing suicide during difficult times in their lives. Zachariah described:

> My kids did play a part in recovery, and because I never wanted to be. . .because there's a lot of times I thought about suicide. Then I thought about my kids. Then my grandkids, about getting better to be better for them, to have something to leave them. I'm always striving, pushing, pushing, pushing, but patiently pushing, taking it step by step, because at the end of the day, I want to be able to leave our kids something, you know?

When asked about decisions that he made because of his role as a father, Joshua said, "Life." When asked to elaborate, Joshua went on to explain:

> Still being here. There was a point in time where I was in a dark place and the thought of ending my life was very in the air and I remember, when I planned it out, I had it all planned out of how I was going to leave, and it was New Year's Eve, and I had just left from my church service. And I had told myself, I said, "Okay, I'm not entering the New Year. I'm not

entering the New Year at all." And I went to church because something told me, "You need to hear the Word. You need to hear your bishop talk." And I went there, and I heard it, but something still was like, "You're still going to do this." Some voice in my head was like, "We're still going through with this." . . . And I went to where I was going to go and I was in my car and I was just sitting there and I was going to reach to open the door to get out to do this, but I felt something pull back and I kept hearing a voice in my head, and the voice was my daughter calling for me. And me consistently hearing that and it overpowered any other voice, it was like I need to be there for her because, if I'm not there for her, my daughter is not going to know how to go on and move on with life.

Joshua also referenced the death of his favorite basketball player Kobe Bryant, and his relationship with his daughter Gianna who died with him in a helicopter crash. Joshua discussed the sentiments of Kobe Bryant's widow as a parallel to his own emotions. He stated:

Those two were inseparable. One couldn't live without the other. It was only fitting, even though selfishly, his wife is like, "I wish they were still here, but I understand that, if one left, the other one wouldn't be the same. They wouldn't be able to function," and that's how I feel with my daughter. I feel like, if something happened to her, I wouldn't know how to function, just like if something happened to me, she wouldn't know how to function."

Thaddeus discussed events surrounding his son's suicide. Although depressed, he was not suicidal himself. However, he recalled being in a dark place, and coming out of it upon a drunken night, and thoughts of his children. Concerning making progress, Thaddeus recalled:

> I'm still throwing a pity party for myself, and I'm getting drunk. I went back to my parents' old house, because we had boarded it up, because nobody was living there, and they had stolen the pipes out of it. So, one of the windows was open and I went in there. Somebody had been squatting. I'm like, "Man, I'm drunk. It's 10:30 at night." So, I'm like, "I'll just tell my brothers in the morning." So, I go back out the window. It caught me by one leg, hanging out the window, about a foot from the ground; couldn't touch the ground. I had a little prayer with God. I said, "Lord, I just lost my son. Now my kids are going to lose their father like this." Somehow, a piece of the house came apart. I came out and I went straight to rehab.

In reference to progress, Joshua also mentioned that his decisions about how involved he would be with his child were based largely on his experience of not having an emotionally or financially supportive father. When asked to describe an instance where his experience as a father impacted life decisions, Joshua went on to explain, "I was like, okay, I need to have a career. I don't want to have a job. I want to have a career." Joshua's feelings on completing college had a lot to do with putting himself in a good financial position to take care of his daughter, as well as lead by example. This is highlighted when Joshua stated:

> I want to show my daughter that she can go forward in school as well. She doesn't have to just stop at high school. She can go on to go to college and not have any fear. That led to that because it was a goal of mine to set the bar for her to see this, to see the success of continuing in education.

Participants described the resiliency and progress in their lives based on fatherhood. Three of the six participants mentioned suicide. Two of those three participants expressed thoughts of their children being the reason why they did not commit suicide during depressive states of mind. The other participant used the tragic suicide of one of his children to show resiliency for the sake of his other children. All six participants spoke about their enrollment status in community college as the perceived catalyst to better careers, more financial resources, and upward social mobility. Each of the six participants spoke about using education as a motivator for their children.

Desire to be living proof. The interview data in this study reinforced the idea that all six participants wanted to prove to themselves, as well as any doubters of their abilities to be good fathers and college graduates. When asked the question, "Can you describe any instances where your experience as a father has impacted life decisions?" two of the six participants talked about forgoing athletic scholarships to different colleges because it would have meant being away from their children. In relation to wanting to be living proof of a responsible Black male who put his children first, Ishmael stated, "I got a scholarship to Morris Brown that I didn't take because I found out that I was having a kid." Since his father was not around when he was a child, he did not hesitate to decline the football scholarship. Ishmael went on to explain, "Yeah, because they wouldn't let his mom or him [the baby] come. And it was just like that." Even though the scholarship would have taken him out of his rough environment, he did not think twice about leaving without his son. Ishmael wanted to prove that he could be the responsible father that he never had. Proof of sacrifice for the sake of his son is what Ishmael described:

> I wasn't going to do it, though, honestly. Because even when I was preparing for my son to come around, it was a struggle. His mom wasn't working, and I was pretty much buying everything. So, I knew if I would've left, then it would've been even worse for him, though.

Like Ishmael, Thaddeus shared a story of sacrifice. He explained:

> I'll give you a little background from when I first was a father. I was a father first when I was 19 years old. I had just graduated from high school, but I had a scholarship to play football. Matter of fact, one of the places that wanted me to play for them was St. John Fisher [College].

Thaddeus continued:

I had a full scholarship to a school in Pennsylvania. But because my son was coming that September, I decided to go full time to work, instead of going and pursuing my football thing, because it's D2 and D3 football. You're not really looking at going to the NFL, but you still had a free education.

In addition to turning down an athletic scholarship, Ismael also relocated to a different city, and left a job opportunity to provide better opportunities for his son. He stated:

I left the fire department so my son can have a better life outside of New York City. I used to work for the fire department. I had 8 years under me, though. And the point was like the way I grew up. . . And New York City doesn't offer anything for kids. And my daughter was up here having a better life. There was like a swimming pool, there was a better opportunity. And then just basically, before we moved up here, my son was pretty much leaning towards trouble, though. So, I thought it would be like a better opportunity for him to get out of the area. I mean, that's what I always wanted, just to get out of the hood. New York City is a hood. But I wanted to get out of the hood. So I left the fire department so I could give him a better life. I moved up here with my wife, and I mean, it's been good ever since. High grades for him, he plays sports. Because there's no sports that you can play in New York City except basketball. They don't offer anything else.

Ishmael spoke about "doing what he needed to do" for the sake of his children. How he felt about his sacrifices were apparent in his statement, "I've already lived my life and I made my decisions, some of them I'm proud of, and some of them I'm not. But I can do better for them."

Participants talked about how being a father shaped their lives and their determination to make a better life for themselves and their children. All six of the participants mentioned wanting to prove to be positive role models for their children. The participants aimed to teach their children that following their father's footsteps could lead to positive outcomes which included college education.

All six participants spoke about using their enrollment in college as a motivator for their children. Thaddeus explained, "My kids are in college, too. So, if I can get the grade, there isn't any reason why you can't!" Thaddeus spoke about being a role model to his children in relation to higher education. He went on to state:

> My daughter, she goes to West Georgia. We compete on the grade level all the time. My oldest son, he's 24. He's out of school. But even with him; don't tell me you can't do it, because Daddy shown you how to do it. Daddy's done it. Let's get it on, and they respect that.

Zion took his experience of being a role model a step further by suggesting that as a non-traditional student, he looked to have a positive impact on younger Black males at the college. According to Zion:

Well, I can see myself more or less mentoring other young men that ain't my child. You see what I'm saying? Help them see some things the same way that I would help my son see some things. And not just about school, but about life. Just living life, and the things that could happen, what your reaction could be, stuff like that.

Zachariah spoke about the desire to be living proof of a Black father who thought about his children's future. Zachariah felt the need to prove to be a living example against negative stereotypes of Black fathers. Through college persistence, Zacharia explained working to build a legacy for his children and grandchildren. As he stated above, "I'm always striving, pushing, pushing, pushing, but patiently pushing, taking it step by step, because at the end of the day, I want to be able to leave our kids something, you know?"

All six participants in this study felt that as Black males, they needed to remove themselves from negative stereotypes such as "deadbeat dads," or people who could not succeed in higher education. Participants felt that negative stereotypes of Black men in general, and Black fathers specifically had given then extra motivation to be successful in fatherhood, education, and career goals. The participants also explained their desire to disassociate from the stereotypical association of Black males with criminal behavior. In addition, the participants also wanted to prove to themselves that they could either continue the pattern of involved fathers in their families, or on the other hand, cease the pattern of uninvolved fathers in their families. All six participants concluded that their children were at the center of their persistence in community college.

Research Question 3. Research Question 3 (RQ3) examined how community colleges support Black student-fathers. Participants reported (a) typical unnecessary obstacles and (b) true acknowledgment and acceptance. The theme of typical unnecessary obstacles included subthemes of lack of support and racism. The themes and subthemes are discussed below. Table 4.5 presents the two themes, two subthemes, and five key concepts that emerged from RQ3.

Table 4.5

RQ3 – Themes, Key Concepts, and Subthemes

Theme	Key Concepts	Subtheme
"Typical Unnecessary Obstacles"	Insults Frustration	Lack of Support
		Racism
"True Acknowledgement and Acceptance"	Inclusion	Diversity Programs

Typical unnecessary obstacles. This theme emerged from participants citing barriers in their institutions that were the same barriers they have been accustomed to facing as Black men in America. When asked the question, "How has being a Black male impacted your experience at the college?" participants made statements such as, "You know how it is," or "I'm used to it" while describing the subthemes of lack of support, negative faculty and staff experiences, and racism.

Lack of support. The subtheme of lack of institutional support for Black student-fathers emerged through participants' explanations of their Black male experience in White-dominated institutions. The question of whether the college had resources for him as a Black male, Zachariah stated, "Oh, definitely not," and added that, "Most of the events that we do at our college are geared towards middle-class White women." To go along with the experience of being a Black male, participants were asked if the college had resources for them as fathers. Thaddeus responded that there was no support targeted for Black fathers at all. He said:

> No. No. No. Not as a father. They've got daycare for mothers with kids, stuff like that. But as a support group for fathers that are going to school, too, they don't have anything like that. Yes, they do have a support group for single mothers. They don't have a support group for single fathers.

In addition to lack of support, Ishmael pointed out that there are no grants to support Black fathers and that Black males are just considered as statistics. When speaking about whether the college had supports for Black males, Ishmael reported:

> No. Honestly, no. From what they say, there's so many grants that help people, but it's not a lot. Because when you ask for help, it's just like, "Whoa, why should

we help you? You should be going to a trade school. It's better to go to a trade school than it is to go to college."

When asked if people other than Black males noticed the lack of funding or would look into it, Ishmael stated, "I mean, there's a few teachers that might do it. But otherwise than that, nobody cares. It's just like you're another number, though."

Participants discussed how lack of support for Black student-fathers within their institutions was considered a typical unnecessary obstacle. One participant emphasized the disparity in supports for mothers and supports for fathers. The participant mentioned that the college had support groups and resources for mothers, but nothing in place for fathers. Another participant pointed out a lack of available grants or financial assistance that is specific to Black student-fathers. Both participants did bring up these issues with no hesitation and a matter of fact temperament, which was consistent with the idea that they were typical issues in terms of their experiences of being overlooked as Black student-fathers.

Racism. This subtheme emerged as participants reported having experienced overt racism, microaggressions, and exclusion from programs. Participants also discussed experiencing discouragement from faculty and staff. These experiences made them believe that the institution was not supporting Black student-fathers. For example, Zion mentioned that there was no support in terms of career or nurturing talents. He recalled the types of responses he has heard when

Black male students attempt to add their perspective to classes. He stated, "A few professors are open, but other professors will be like, 'Well, I'm the professor, and you need to. . .' suggesting that Black student perspectives were not always welcome."

Zion also mentioned that one of the few Black staff members at the college tried to help Black male students, but his efforts were not supported. Zion said:

> He more or less uses his resources to help them. But the college itself really don't promote that. And sometimes they have gotten angry with the director for doing what he do. Some of the people at school, they don't like that. There was even one guy, he was an athlete raising a son. And he couldn't play basketball. Then there was another one that couldn't play football or whatever. And so, the school was not encouraging enough, so they dropped out.

Adding support to the subtheme of racism, Ishmael gave an example of an experience he had with counseling staff in terms of selecting appropriate courses for his career goals. During the interaction, he recalled an instance where he was insulted by prejudice. He reported the condescending nature of some college employees. As a Black student-father, he had often felt disrespected and angered by the assumptions that he could not succeed in certain programs: Ishmael explained:

> Like a guidance counselor. Like basically, when you're talking to a guidance counselor and you go,

"Oh, I want to look into this, and I want to be in a PA program." And they'll pretty much stare at you for a minute and just say, "But you can do something else besides being in a PA program. You can do automotive or you can go to a school where you can be a mechanic." You know?

Participants discussed how negative staff experiences due to racism were typical unnecessary obstacles. One participant expressed that most faculty did not give Black male students a voice in classes during discussions and were disinterested in their perspectives. The participant also mentioned that a Black faculty member who utilized his own funds to assist Black male students was reprimanded by his college citing a boundary issue. Another participant pointed out being looked down upon by a guidance counselor who suggested he try trade school instead of a physician's assistant program. Again, these participants did not dwell on these issues, as they were consistent with the idea that they were typical in terms of their experiences of being overlooked as Black men.

Participants also discussed being discriminated against in different situations. These participants expressed the institutional racism at their respective colleges. When asked about how being a Black male impacted his experience at the college Thaddeus described:

> So, we may be experiencing a lot of institutional racism, but I don't really think it's a lot of interpersonal racism. But I believe that institutional

racism, because there is this picture of one of the basketball players, and it's like the way they darkened it out. I know they were trying to use the fisheye thing, the fisheye lens effect, and it darkened everything around her so much you can't even see her on the wall, and she was the NJCAA player of the year for that year. Now I know if she was a White girl, there ain't no way that they would allow that to happen.

Thaddeus also mentioned different treatment toward Black male student-athletes. He described the experience by stating:

The basketball players: because they play basketball, they're not holding them to the same level as the regular people. I think that's going to hurt them in the long run. Now, as in, one of the things that does concern me is that they don't have a Black history class, or anything of that situation. We've been talking about it for a while, and it hasn't happened since I've been there, and I'm about to graduate.

Ishmael reflected on his perspective of some of the professors at his college. He said:

Well, some teachers will be like, "Well, I'm going to be honest with you. You're either going to fail out and then you're probably going to come back. That's what usually students do. Like usually, basically, what you [Black] students do is, for the first time you come to college, you usually fail out."

Participants discussed experiencing racism through Black students being excluded from certain programs and being discriminated against in various situations. One participant expressed the frustration that he felt knowing that some instructors expect Black students to fail and leave the institution before being successful and completing their degree. The condescending nature of faculty towards Black students was understood as par for the course. Another participant described how his institution was doing Black student-athletes a disservice by not holding them accountable as academic students.

True acknowledgement and acceptance. This theme emerged from participants' suggestions for what can promote inclusive excellence at their respective institutions. All six participants had suggestions about what their colleges could do to assist Black student-fathers. Some suggestions targeted Black males in general, and some suggestions targeted Black fathers.

Participants responded to the question, "What could the college do to increase the success of Black student-fathers?" In addressing Black males in general, Joshua suggested that his college hire more professors with whom Black male students could identify. He stated, "For one, have more Black professors there." Thaddeus corroborated Joshua's response. When asked the same question addressing what the college could do to support Black student-fathers, Thaddeus stated, "Black male faculty." Although Thaddeus felt the same as Joshua in terms of having more Black faculty at his college, he added more depth.

Thaddeus brought up recruitment efforts for more Black students in addition to Black male faculty. He explained, "They need to get more into the community. Even with the events that we have in the city, if they want more diversity in the school, they're going to have to get into the community." Thaddeus described how another local college had much more presence in the community to attract and recruit Black students. He even mentioned that his college did not appear to be interested in the recruitment of Black students. Thaddeus recalled a time when he tried to get the college involved in community engagement, but could not get any assistance. According to Thaddeus:

> It seems like they're not interested in the urban life. That's why you're not going to get the diversity that you want in the school. Because if you're not sponsoring anything in the high schools, why are they going to come to your school? They don't even really know about you. So, that's the type of things I would like for them to get more involved. I even tried to get them involved in one. I tried to get them to sponsor a table at a community event. They didn't even give me a response back.

Some participants made suggestions their colleges could implement for Black student-fathers. For example, Zion suggested "They could provide the same resources to the Black male fathers that they provide to the single mothers." Some participants focused on programming. Zachariah mentioned the possibility of free fatherhood class for minorities. Joshua had the following suggestion:

Have some program where alumni can come back and be somewhat of a mentor to other fathers, and help them get through whatever they have to get through. Even if they need just someone to talk to, to vent, to get whatever they need to get out, or have some type of guidance.

Ishmael suggested:

Start a group. You know, I didn't have a dad. So if you start a group and somebody else that had a dad, and they could be like, "Well, I went through that problem. I can show you what's the process of getting through there. Like I can relate to somebody else."

Participants discussed the desire to have true acknowledgment, and acceptance from their institutions. When asked what their schools could do to support Black male student-fathers, some participants focused on what could be done to support Black males in general. Other participants talked about what could be done for Black student-fathers.

In support of Black males in general, participants talked about their institutions putting in a sincere effort to recruit, and hire more Black male instructors. In addition to recruiting more Black faculty, one participant also expressed the need for his community college actually to get into the community to recruit Black students.

In support of Black student-fathers, participants pointed out the need for their institution to have programs tailored toward them, just as they do for women. Another participant mentioned the need for support groups where experienced fathers can offer guidance to those who may need it. These items were suggested responses to making Black student-fathers feel acknowledged and supported. All six participants concluded that support systems in community colleges are lacking for Black student-fathers.

COMPOSITE TEXTURAL DESCRIPTION

In the composite textural description, the themes are examined and used to articulate the whole group experience (Moustakas, 1994). The composited textural description articulated the collective description of Black fathers' perception of their own and their father's fatherhood impacts persistence in community college. The themes discussed above represented the data that Using the above themes, the data describing the experience of growing as a child, living as a father, and having different college experiences as a Black man.

The participants' experiences of fatherhood were examined from their perspectives of being sons going through childhood and as fathers raising children. Regarding childhood experiences, four of the six participants believed they had responsible fathers who made sure they would have a better life in the future. Participants used words and phrases like "care," "help," "responsibility," "product of his father," "support," and "determined" to describe their experiences with healthy parenting from their fathers. Participants felt that learning parenting skills from their fathers helped them build confidence and laid a foundation for being responsible Black fathers to their children. Participants acknowledged that many Black fathers are absent from their children's lives and conveyed the importance and appreciation of having fathers who were available to them.

The two participants who did not have their fathers present on a consistent basis as children believed that they had irresponsible fathers who were not concerned with how their son's lives turned out. They also acknowledged the absence of many Black fathers in their children's lives and expressed the shame, frustration, and embarrassment they felt for being part of that statistic. The two participants used words and phrases like "mistakes," "complete strangers," "wasn't there," "winging it," and "once in a blue moon" to describe their experiences with unhealthy parenting from their fathers. These two participants felt that the lack of relationship with their fathers caused them to feel insecure, unsupported, and susceptible to negative influences. These feelings made them work hard to be responsible Black fathers to their children.

Participants were equally likely to nurture, support, advise, and be present for their children whether their fathers were present for them growing up or not. Four of the six participants were able to learn how to be supportive fathers directly. Two out of the six participants described how they had to learn how to be supportive fathers in a more indirect manner. They explained that they took all the painful things that they experienced as children and aimed to do the opposite for their children. All six participants felt like experiencing fatherhood from a son's perspective prepared them for their own experience of fatherhood.

Regarding their own experiences as fathers, all six participants expressed feelings of wanting to be responsible fathers who were role models to their children. Participants used words and phrases such as "determined," "sacrifice," "role model," "go forward," and "proving" to describe their attitudes toward raising their children. Participants reported being a father as the key to persistence in life economically, socially, and most importantly, their pursuit of education at their college.

All six participants expressed the desire to lay a better foundation for their children in terms of education and the ability to support them for a better future. Furthermore, some participants mentioned falling into alcohol and drug use and marital separations. However, due to their experiences of fatherhood and thoughts of their children, they were able to reform and persist. The participants' status as Black men, a historically maligned and marginalized demographic, served as an underlying motivation to be great fathers. Participants believed that working against the negative stereotypes of Black fathers gave them extra strength when difficulties arose. This extra boost came from the desire to prove to themselves and American society, at large in America that Black males can handle their responsibilities as fathers, and not succumb to alcohol, drug use, or incarceration.

Regarding persistence in community college, participants experienced struggles with typical unnecessary obstacles and wanting to have true acknowledgment and acceptance from their institutions. Participants highlighted that much of their success in college was due to their role as fathers, as well as how they were brought up by their parents. Many participants showed determination and desire to learn, shape their careers, and be positive examples for their children.

The participants' status as Black males was more openly recognized in their educational settings than in the context of fatherhood. Despite negative criticism and lack of support from the institutions they attended, they showed resilience. Participants stated some professors were of no help since they believed Black students had a higher probability of failing compared to the White students. Just as in fatherhood, negative stereotypes and low expectations hang over the heads of Black men, such as the case with education. The participants used these negative views as motivation to remain successful in college just as they were motivated to be good fathers. Additionally, participants felt that their children were paramount to their success in life and persistence in community college completion.

COMPOSITE STRUCTURAL DESCRIPTION

As stated above, the composite textural description communicates the total group experience. The composite structural description describes how the participants experienced the phenomenon (Moustakas, 1994). The structural descriptions focused on the background stories of the participants. The issue of college experience was paramount when examining the phenomenon of how Black male students perceive fatherhood (their own and their fathers') and how it impacts their persistence in community college. Many participants arrived in college through their love of learning and desire to learn and obtain degrees in higher education.

All six participants reported a desire to pursue higher education and build a career. Most participants felt that higher education was the gateway to better opportunities. Participants also believed their status as college students sets a good example for their children as they grow up.

The six participants demonstrated the belief that difficult past experiences do not have to be a hindrance to progression. Participants are also of the belief that the institution has a significant impact on their ability to persist. Participants revealed negative staff experiences that affected some of their Black colleagues; however, despite these negative experiences, some participants were able to have a positive mindset and perform better.

Participants recalled professors who were open to responding to their questions, which helped them to perform better. Participants who had positive experiences with staff explained that their fair treatment was also due to their personality as opposed to race. Unfortunately, there were also cases of racism. Participants recalled staff treating them as if they could not be successful in academia and should instead pursue trade school. Participants also talked about faculty doing Black male student-athletes a disservice by not holding them to the standards that they hold White students as if to say that they are only valuable for sports. Participants also communicated the lack of activities, events, and supports that appeal to Black student's cultural backgrounds.

TEXTURAL STRUCTURAL SYNTHESIS

Textural structural synthesis is "an integration of the composite textural and composite structural descriptions, providing a synthesis of the meanings and essences of the experience (Moustakas, 1994, p. 144). Participants had a long history of parenting, fatherhood, and how they ended up in college. Lack of money, strict parenting, lack of father figures, and becoming a father at earlier ages solidified goals to pursue higher education. Furthermore, participants recalled specific negative experiences demoralized and demotivated them, such as their own lack of a supportive father, and projected beliefs from outsiders that Black men are failures and belong to trade schools.

Participants hesitated to enroll in college or university because they believed their obligation was to look for jobs to support their children. Some participants mentioned great sponsors, institutions, and professors who helped them continue with their college-level education. Although participants were determined to continue with their college goals, negative experience, self-doubt, and about what they want in life were prevalent among participants.

Initial success in their persistence in achieving higher education was mostly clouded by lack of money, fatherhood responsibilities, and beliefs that Blacks students fail. Participants quickly pointed out that there was a lack of institutional support for the success of Black student-fathers. Participants sought out Black faculty and staff in search of academic and emotional support. Collectively, participants did not like the way they were treated by their professors or regarded by the institution.

CONCLUSION

Through semi-structured interviews, six participants shared their lived experience of being Black male community college students with children. The themes that emerged from the data were (a) healthy parenting, (b) unhealthy parenting, (c) impenetrable connections, (d) resilience, and progress, (e) desire to be living proof, (f) typical unnecessary obstacles, and (g) true acknowledgment and acceptance.

Two themes emerged from the first research question that examined how Black male college students experience fatherhood (from a son's perspective) facilitating or impeding community college completion. The themes of healthy parenting and unhealthy parenting emerged from participants' stories of their fathers being present, involved, supportive, and responsible, or absent, disengaged, and unsupportive. Participants who experienced healthy parenting from their fathers appreciated and respected the lessons and examples. They looked to instill the same values in their children. Participants who experienced unhealthy parenting from their fathers used the memory of their struggles as motivation to make sure that their children did not have to experience those feelings.

Three themes emerged from the second research question that examined how Black male college students experience fatherhood (from a father's perspective) facilitating or impeding community college completion. The themes of impenetrable connection emerged from participants' stories of experiencing the births of their children and using its concomitant joy and fear to focus on the task of being a good father. Participants also recalled times when they were in awe of their children when they were present for certain experiences and shared moments.

The theme of resilience and progress emerged from participants sharing their experiences of persisting in college to be good role models for the children. Participants also recounted times when the very thought of their children prevented them from harmful acts or delving deeper into addiction. Participants spoke of progress, especially in the cases where they did not have guidance as children.

The theme of wanting to be living proof emerged from participants sharing their stories of sacrificing educational opportunities, job opportunities, and relocation to better support their children. Participants mentioned wanting to prove to themselves, as well as to society, that Black men can do what needs to be done to break the stereotype of "deadbeat dad." Participants also wanted to show their children that they can also be successful in college.

Two themes emerged from the third research question that examined how community colleges support Black students who are fathers (in the experience of Black male students). The themes typical unnecessary obstacles and true acknowledgment and acceptance emerged from participant stories of lack of support, negative experiences with faculty, and staff, racism, lack of diversity, and need for culturally specific programs. These experiences have caused frustration with their institutions by feeling discriminated against and unwanted.

As mentioned in Chapter 3, the final step in transcendental phenomenological analysis is textural-structural synthesis (Moustakas, 1994). The above-mentioned themes and subthemes were extracted from the participants' lived experiences and synthesized. The overall essence of "what" and the "how" of the phenomenon is expressed through three key findings (Moustakas, 1994).

First, fatherhood acts as a catalyst to community college completion for Black student-fathers. This is based on four of the six participants expressing the appreciation for having responsible, involved fathers to help motivate them to complete college. This finding is also based on two of the six participants expressing the inner drive to complete college that evolved within them due to the frustrations of having uninvolved or absent fathers.

The second finding is that children are at the center of persistence for Black student-fathers. This is based on all six participants expressing how the thought of their children is what keeps them motivated to persist in college, even during challenges such as depression, anger and frustrations that come with being Black men in America. All participants stated that they wanted to be role models for their children, as well as wanting to be in a better position economically to better assist their children.

The third finding is that support systems in community colleges are lacking for Black student-fathers. This is based on all six participants expressing that they feel invisible as Black student-fathers. Participants stated that the lack of programming and supports specific to Black student-fathers proves to them their institutions do not recognize them or choose not to acknowledge them. This chapter discussed the findings for this study. Chapter 5 discusses the findings and their implications, as well as recommendations for future research.

CHAPTER 5

DISCUSSION

INTRODUCTION

The purpose of this study was to gain a better understanding of how Black fathers' perception of their own and their father's fatherhood impacts persistence in community college. This inquiry was framed in the notion of "lived experience" (Moustakas, 1994), that is, the phenomenology of being a Black father and student at an American community college. Throughout the study, the motivations, anxieties, and embodied experiences as Black men and fathers came to light. How these particular embodied experiences are regarded, supported, or discouraged by the institutional structure of the colleges they attend and the actors who constitute the institution and its community were also examined.

The research questions sought to unpack the experience of Black student-fathers by articulating their experience with fatherhood with their experience as students. These dual roles can serve as impediments as well as facilitators to the goals the subjects pursued in both contexts. Further, within the context of the institution, these goals were also challenged.

This study endeavored to approach these issues with a three-pronged approach: the interstices between higher education, fatherhood, and being a Black man in the United States. These intersections yield a unique paradigm of experience and one which is constantly in tension with the larger society and its institutions. For example, community colleges provide students easy access to the college environment for the purposes of educational attainment and other socioeconomic opportunities (Brand et al., 2014; Goldrick-Rab, 2010), which are strongly correlated with achieving better socioeconomic outcomes. On the other hand, Black men are statistically among the least likely to achieve postsecondary degrees, with complicated reasons for this pattern. Meanwhile, many Black men become fathers, and because of the particular constellation of challenges facing Black men, which includes education access and quality, disparate rates of incarceration, lower socioeconomic status (which can preclude access to higher education), their children have higher rates of being raised in single-mother homes and concomitant higher rates of poverty (Duncan et al., 2014).

Given this constellation of factors and outcomes that are part of the experience of being a Black man in the United States, the literature on persistence in higher education cannot fully reflect Black men's perceptions and experiences of how fatherhood impacts community college completion. Several themes emerged from the key findings that elaborate on this argument.

FINDINGS AND IMPLICATIONS

As stated in Chapter 4, the essence of how Black students experience their own and their father's fatherhood and how it impacts persistence in community college is expressed through three key findings. First, fatherhood acts as a catalyst to community college completion for Black student-fathers. Second, children are at the center of persistence for Black student-fathers. Third, support systems in community colleges are lacking for Black student-fathers.

Fatherhood is a catalyst to community college completion. Stereotypes of generations of Black males being raised without a father in the home are pervasive in American society (Cooper et al., 2020). Stereotypes about Black males being uneducated are also insinuated through the ignorance of the structural issues that have created formidable obstacles to achieving education that other racial groups do not encounter (Cooper et al.,

2012). Incarceration statistics, education statistics, media portrayals, generalizations, Black male education data, and assumptions about Black fatherhood exacerbate these ideas (Allen, 2016; Alexander, 2012). However, the interview data in this study explain things differently.

Parenting matters. Parenting was a main theme that emerged from the data, and in particular, whether parenting is or was "healthy" or "unhealthy," which in most cases referred to the presence or absence of the parent in the home and whether parents made a meaningful effort toward providing financial support. As discussed in Chapter 1, past studies that focused on Black fathers' (or lack thereof) involvement, and the outcomes for children (Gordon et al., 2013). This study shares that objective and takes it a step further by assessing the duality of fatherhood in Black men, that is, their experience as a son and as a father.

Participants who experienced healthy parenting from their fathers explained how their fathers worked hard to support the family. This was expressed by participants in circumstances whether their fathers made a comfortable living or merely made enough to get by. That is, the effort was more critical than monetary sums. Studies such as Cooper et al. (2020) outline the attitudes and behaviors of involved Black fathers. This study aimed to do the same.

Participants who experienced unhealthy parenting from their fathers had financial struggles due in part to their fathers not contributing to the household consistently. These struggles served as an inspiration for them to enroll and persist in college as a way of obtaining higher socioeconomic status in adulthood. Strayhorn (2015) observes that participants who had financial hardships used the experience as motivation to attend college as a catalyst for a better financial situation. Consistent with Strayhorn's research, this study concluded that Black student-fathers viewed college as a necessary step to position themselves to be better off financially for the benefit of themselves and their children.

The noncognitive domain (Wood & Harris, 2012) speaks to the emotional responses to social interactions based on a person's environment. In line with Wood and Harris's work, the theme of healthy parenting in this study included discipline, responsibility, and effort on the part of the participants' fathers. From the participants' environment (as sons), they took pieces of certain characteristics of their fathers' fatherhood and made them their own. This was reflected in the statement of taking various strategies to become a "Shaolin master" of fatherhood by one of the participants.

Conversely, the emotional responses of Black males without father figures, or marginally involved father figures, had a deeper journey to what they considered fatherhood mastery. Participants who experienced unhealthy parenting from their fathers learned what they should not do as opposed to learning what they should do. Orrock and Clark (2018) found that a lack of positive role models increased the likelihood of lowering academic confidence. Contrary to the findings of Orrock and Clark (2018), this study found that lack of father involvement can result in positives such as personal drive, resiliency, and inspiration to become successful, educated fathers.

The noncognitive domain (Wood & Harris, 2012) also includes self-efficacy. As described in Chapter 2 under self-efficacy, participants in Strayhorn's (2015) study used words and phrases like "confidence" and "feel like I can do it" to describe the internal forces that motivated them. This study is consistent with Strayhorn's research as participants used similar words and phrases in such as "determined" and "go forward" in relation to both completing community college and being good fathers. Based on the findings of this study, it should be noted that Black males who grew up without the involvement of a father, or fathers who did not display healthy parenting, should not be written off as people who cannot become successful in education or fatherhood.

The data from this study found that whether or not Black males experience healthy parenting or unhealthy parenting from their fathers, it is a driving force behind their persistence in community college. Chapter 2 outlines Holliday and Strange (2017) discussed the importance of male role models to Black male persistence. However, Holliday and Strange (2017) spoke about role models being pastors, coaches, and famous figures. This study was consistent with Holliday and Strange's study as far as the importance of male role models for Black male persistence. However, this study differed from Holliday and Strange's research as the important male role models in this study were Black fathers.

Participants in this study who experienced healthy parenting from their fathers appreciated it and looked to provide the same for their children. Conversely, Black fathers who experienced unhealthy parenting from their fathers used that struggle as motivation to do right by their own children. The participants experienced the pain and suffering that came with the lack or loss of a father figure in their lives. This is consistent with Black males' feelings of low self-esteem due to the lack of a positive male role model (Orrock & Clark, 2018).

Both healthy and unhealthy parenting facilitated community college completion as part of being a positive example for their children. All six participants understood the importance of being positive role models as fathers and Black men. As noted in Chapter 2, Brooks' (2015) study found that students' motivation to succeed came from the goal of being a role model for other family members. This is consistent with the findings in this study as the participants worked hard to make sure their children had a strong Black father (role model) to look up to. What differed between the two studies is that participants in Brooks' (2015) study wanted to set examples for their siblings and extended family members, whereas participants in this study sought to set the precedent for their children.

Children are at the center of persistence for Black student-fathers. The connection Black fathers have with their children is strong enough to summon resilience in hard times, as well as encourage progress in terms of career, and educational attainment. All six participants learned from a son's perspective on how to be, or not be, good fathers. Exploring the research question from a father's perspective presented the themes of impenetrable lifelong connections, resilience and progress, and desire to be living proof.

Impenetrable lifelong connections. The literature review discusses social support as a factor for persistence as a part of Wood and Harris's (2012) environmental domain. In Anumba's 2015 study, social support included the impact of family structure, and relationships, on the academic outcomes of Black college students. In this study, impenetrable lifelong connection was the theme that linked this study to social support as a factor for persistence. All six participants in this study focused on their heightened connectivity to their children. The Black fathers in this study understood the importance of being a social support for their children, while recognizing the benefits of their children being supports for them.

All six participants reported that the very thought of their children got them through difficult times, and as such, their children served as a form of social support. While the children may not have known how their existence provided motivation and support to their fathers, the fact that their fathers experienced their children as a personal resource and moral support shows that the children were considered a critical source of support. In this study, the difficult times that were expressed ranged from stress in school to suicidal ideations. This is significant because a lack of support has resulted in emotional struggles for these men. As mentioned earlier, Wood and Harris's (2012) noncognitive domain speaks to the emotional responses to a person's environment. Some participants in this study did not have a present father figure growing up and the experience shaped their emotional responses. Participants' statements such as "I didn't have that figure in life, like that father figure to tell me, 'Well, do this with your son' or 'Do that for your son'" corroborates the idea of an emotional response to a person's environment according to Wood and Harris (2012). Fortunately, participants have become fathers and now have the experience of receiving that support from their children. In Chapter 1, data from the National Fatherhood Initiative (2018) reported children with present fathers are less likely to face abuse and neglect, less likely to commit crimes and become incarcerated. Results from participant interviews reflect knowledge of that data with statements such as, "I'm her protector. If anything happens to her, I'm possibly going to jail, because that's my daughter."

Further, all six participants reported that their drive to support for their children also provides the strength for them to persist in college. Chapter 2 discusses Wood and Williams' (2013) study, which outlined family responsibilities as "environmental pull." When comparing the results of this study to the findings of Wood and Williams' research, it must be pointed out that family responsibility, for these participants, was more of a "push" towards college completion than a "pull" (away from). Participants felt that their responsibility to their children is what kept them moving forward even when support was minimal at their institutions. The theme of impenetrable lifelong connections relates directly to the theme of resilience and progress.

Resilience and progress. The theme of resilience and progress spoke to the participants' deep dives into their own self-reflection to keep working towards putting themselves and their children in a better position. Five of the six participants described experiences where they felt like giving up on school, relationships, and in two separate cases, life itself. One participant recalled hearing his daughter's voice as he contemplated suicide while sitting in his car. Like the other five participants, his child was at the center of his persistence, not just for college, but for life itself. This substantiates Durkheim's (1897) suicide theory that posited that suicide is more likely to occur in individuals who are not well integrated into society. This participant was well integrated into society and had a powerful father-child connection. He made it through that difficult time because of the thought of his daughter, and now he is a healthy, strong-minded, honors student in college owing to the centering of his daughter in his moving forward.

Desire to be living proof. The third theme under this finding was the desire to be living proof. All six participants stated that they wanted to prove to themselves and their children that they could complete college. Five of the six participants also stated that they wanted to prove to people outside of themselves and their children that they could complete college. The study participants often feel as if they need to work to dispel negative stereotypes. This is consistent with Cooper et al.'s (2020) study that states, "Analyses found a number of implicit and explicit motivations for African American fathers' parenting strategies" (p. 71).

Participants also wanted to prove to themselves, their children, and society that they could be good fathers. The effort to dispel stereotypes often complicates Black male identity (Cooper, 2013). This is consistent with the study by Boyd and Mitchell (2018), which states Black males need to utilize different skill sets to persist against negative stereotypes. Participants in this study were no different. This was evidenced by the plethora of sacrifices made, such as foregoing athletic scholarships and relocating for the sake of staying close to their children.

The participants in this study were involved fathers. Maintaining that status was a way to combat the stereotype of Black men as uninvolved fathers. More importantly, they maintained their involvement because they wanted to be there for the children they loved. Their dedication went far beyond using the children as a prop to disprove a stereotype assigned to them by American society. The consensus is that two-parent households are ideal for children (Orrock & Clark, 2018), but the odds of achieving this ideal are compromised for Black men due to racism and incarceration rates, so Black families and communities face unique challenges as a result.

Participants working to complete their college education was a way to combat the stereotype of Black men being uneducated. However, one participant stated that he did not care what anybody outside of his immediate family thought about him, and that he did not need to prove anything to anybody. Incidentally, the participant did not grow up in the United States and did not have the same experiences as the Black American males. This provides some corroboration to the argument of Black American men internalizing negative stereotypes from their society (Boyd & Mitchell, 2018).

Although one participant had a different approach from the other five, all six participants expressed a positive self-image. As participants ages ranged from 31 to 56 years old, their positive image came from maturity, experience, and overcoming challenges of being Black men in America. This relates to Cross et al.'s (1991) study that posits that Black men start with a neutral to negative attitude about their race, which persists, or can be transformed to positive by life experiences. There was no evidence in this study to suggest that participants had a neutral or negative attitude about being Black. The fathers in this study were comfortable in their own skin as Black men in America despite experiencing stereotypes and prejudices. Participants became comfortable at different times in their lives after opportunities for growth from mistakes, successes, and the love for and from their children. This level of comfort is what partially made it possible for them to pursue a college degree. Finding success in the community college space despite the struggles described in this study has contributed to that comfort.

Their experiences related to the theme of desire to be living proof spoke to the overt discrimination and microaggressions that they faced as Black student-fathers. For example, when a participant was told that he should consider enrolling in a trade program as opposed to an academic program, he made it a point to prove to the "advisor" that he could excel at whatever he put his mind to. Boyd and Mitchell's (2018) study found that participants experienced microaggressions and normalization or acceptance of Black male stereotypes. Similarly, participants in this study experienced microaggressions in their community colleges that consisted of examples such as being warned that they may not be successful on their first try in college, or conversely, being praised in a shocked fashion when they are seen to be involved fathers as to imply that they should not be. "Precisely, being a Black father often comes with a great deal of ridicule, criticism, and stereotypical verbosity that consistently challenges the paternal role" (Lemmons & Johnson, 2019, p. 88). In the case of these participants, these challenges came from the White mainstream society and the White-dominated power structures of their institutions (Fornili, 2018; Levin et al., 2013; Temin, 2017).

All six participants spoke about the power of promoting college completion to their children and role modeling the resilience to follow through. This supports Brooks's (2015) study highlighting that family members communicated the importance of attending college from childhood. All six participants in this study were nontraditional students and wanted their children to attend college earlier in life than they had. All six participants also reported that their fathers did not have a college degree and wanted to establish a new trend for education in their lineage.

Support systems in community colleges are lacking for Black student-fathers. To support Black students who are also fathers, community colleges need to improve efforts at inclusivity to foster inclusion and support for these students. Wood and Harris (2012) describe the institutional domain, which includes campus programs, policies, and practices, and the academic domain, which includes student-faculty interactions, utilization of academic services, student study habits. As described in the literature review, these two domains are similar, but the key difference level of responsibility. The academic domain focuses on the students' responsibility to utilize the college's services, while the institutional domain focuses on the college's responsibility to offer adequate programs and services to the students (Wood & Harris, 2012). Five of the six participants in this study revealed that there were no programs in their institutions for Black student-fathers. In fact, when exploring how community colleges support Black student-fathers, the themes of typical unnecessary obstacles and true acknowledgment and acceptance were unearthed.

Typical unnecessary obstacles. Participants revealed that although the obstacles they faced in their institutions were frustrating, they were written off as the type of typical unnecessary obstacles that they face as Black men in America. The idea that these instances occur so often that they are ignored was consistent with Boyd and Mitchell's (2018) study that discusses Black students ignoring stereotypes. This was evident in one participant's statement, "You know how it is," a shorthand to say that we "Black men" are used to unsavory treatment and it happens so often that it is not a big deal. It was automatically assumed that the researcher's status as a Black man meant that he clearly understood the type of common, aggravating hurdles that Black men face on a regular basis that just get ignored.

The subthemes lack of support and racism emerged under the theme of typical unnecessary obstacles. The literature review outlines support systems within the institution as a key proponent for Black male persistence. The results in this study state that community colleges lack support structures for Black student-fathers as the theme of typical unnecessary obstacles emerged in the data. This is consistent with the research of Strayhorn et al. (2017) that found that Black students spoke about wanting better support in counseling, tutoring, and other on-campus supports. Support systems include networks that provide Black males with the social capital that is critical to their persistence in higher education (Anumba, 2015). According to Harper (2012), social capital refers to the networks of people that can help students navigate the higher education process. Findings in Anumba's research posited that success in college is a group effort as opposed to an individual one. For successful outcomes, a theme that emerged was establishing networks and connections. Participants in this study do not feel supported as Black student-fathers and that that significant category to which they belong is invisible to their institutions.

The subtheme of racism emerged from the data through stories such as participants looking to enroll in academic programs and having to endure propositions to join trade programs instead. A consistent theme within the literature reviewed in Chapter 2 was that Black males face challenges such as insecurity in their identity, racism, and lack of support (Glenn, 2003; Mason, 1998). Black males are more dissatisfied with the campus climate than other ethnic groups (Bush & Bush, 2010). The findings in this study align with those previous findings.

True acknowledgement and acceptance. Participants spoke about the frustrations of not feeling identified as fathers or respected as Black men in their institutions. The theme of true acknowledgment and acceptance emerged in the data and spoke about a lack of trust. Trust in their institution is a significant factor in the academic success of Black males (Rhoden, 2017), yet the experiences participants had during their postsecondary academic careers thwarted such trust more than fostered it, and arguably, by extension, their possibility for academic success was disparately compromised. In other words, lack of trust in the institution compromises academic achievement.

Black fathers are invisible as real, living breathing people on community college campuses. Stereotypes lead others to presume that they are not involved in their children's lives. When they are involved with their children, after all, they are overlooked and dismissed as outliers that do not fit into any comfortable "box" on the campus. Indeed, support systems and programs in community colleges are often present for mothers who are students, but lacking for the fathers who are students.

RECOMMENDATIONS FOR PRACTICE

Four key recommendations for practice emerged from the findings related to how Black fathers' perception of their own and their father's fatherhood impacts persistence in community college. Unlike previous studies on Black male persistence (Anumba, 2015; Holliday & Strange, 2013; Mason, 1998; Strayhorn et al., 2017; Wood & Harris, 2012; Wood & Williams, 2013), recommendations for practices were informed by the voice of the participants. Black student-fathers are not a widely studied population in terms of persistence. However, Black males are recognized as a vulnerable population in college persistence (Harris & Wood, 2013; Wood & Turner, 2011). This study pointed out that some Black male students in higher education are also fathers, thus facing prejudices from two domains: that against Black fathers as absentee and those assumptions about Black men, intellect, and education.

Participants expressed frustration related to the lack of recognition and inclusion, as well as having to function in an environment where they continuously face being negatively judged, labeled, and stereotyped. Unlike participants in studies such as Gumperz (1977), participants in this study did not resort to code switching to dispel stereotypes. Instead, they summoned their inner strength and focus on their children to persist. Based on the findings of this study, the researcher offers the following recommendations for practice.

Community colleges need to recognize Black student-fathers. Black student-fathers feel like they are invisible. This is evidenced by participant data as well as the lack of empirical research on this population. This is a specific group of people who need a support system available within the somewhat unhelpful and prejudiced institutions. For community colleges to recognize Black student-fathers, the researcher recommends that institutions balance support services. For example, if supports are in place or are recommended to assist students with children, they should include fathers as well as mothers. Flyers and signage that advertise these services should feature pictures of Black student-fathers and include them in the verbiage.

Additionally, community colleges should create and maintain committees and task forces to assist in the development and support of Black student-fathers. As stated in foundational persistence literature (Spady, 1970; Tinto, 1975), institutional integration is a factor for persistence. Community colleges' recognition of Black student-fathers acknowledges the student racial identity and identity as a parent. Students who report high levels of institutional integration and positive racial identity earn better grades in college (Reid, 2013). These actions will create a more inclusive environment and promote interaction and relationships between students, as well as between students, faculty, and staff. In turn, this could reduce negative stereotyping that occurs on campus and have a positive impact on Black male persistence through the college milieu, not to mention the overall campus climate. Support systems and tight-knit community connections are key to Black male student persistence (Strayhorn et al., 2017).

Community colleges need to implement support programs specific to Black student-fathers. Community colleges should implement support programs specific to Black student-fathers into their strategic plans. In addition, community colleges should actively seek Black student-fathers to participate in focus groups to give them a voice to communicate what they need from the institution. As a complement to the above recommendation, the promotion of Black student-father programs and active recruitment of Black student-fathers for input will make them feel recognized and supported.

It will also create "buy-in" and a fostering of trust, which will increase student engagement. Black male students are less likely to meet with faculty, advisors, or counselors outside of the classroom (Bush & Bush, 2010). This is consistent with the finding in this study as Black student-fathers clearly communicated that they do not get much out of their institution other than academics, as they do not feel connected with the institution and its community at large.

Programming for student-mothers in community colleges offers support to improve retention, graduation, and employment rates. Some colleges include programming for low-income single mothers attending the institutions. In general, student-mother programs in community colleges also offer nontangible, but valuable support, such as mentorship, case management, career readiness, and job placement, resources that would benefit student-fathers just as much.

Funding, campus presence, and advertising are essential for programming. These should be secured for Black fatherhood-driven activities, mentorship opportunities, and trainings for this population. Parenting programs in community colleges should not only focus on mothers. This is consistent with recommendations from Bush and Bush's (2010) study on Black male achievement in community colleges that noted that institutions need to incorporate culturally and politically relevant campus programming and supports for Black men.

Community colleges need to actively recruit Black male faculty, support staff, and administrators. Since community colleges need first to recognize that Black student-fathers exist as a student population, there should be an understanding that Black student-fathers need to feel like they belong. As stated in Chapter 1, Black males struggle with their sense of belonging (Brooms, 2019). A sense of belonging is fostered by visible representation in the campus community (Strayhorn et al., 2012), that is, Black student-fathers being able to see successful Black males like themselves with academic, administrative, and support roles on campus. Such representation would confer confidence, deeper interest and engagement, a level of social and intellectual comfort, and of course, a sense of belonging to the campus community, rather than feeling like, and being considered, outliers and anomalies.

Hiring Black male faculty, support staff, and administrators should be included in the institution's equity and diversity plan. However, the plan should not stand without active efforts at recruitment. There should be a budget in place for a hiring campaign for the employment of Black males in leadership roles at the college. A search firm should be retained as a neutral party to lead the efforts.

Unlike studies such as Brooks (2015), whose participants were mostly second-generation college students, five of the six participants in this study were first-generation college students. The mother of one participant had attended college. Therefore, no participants in this study had a father figure to help them navigate the higher education environment, demands, and expectations. More Black males in faculty roles and positions of authority may help Black student-fathers feel more comfortable. One of the most consistent themes stemming from the persistence literature on Black male students is the crucial nature of formal and informal student-faculty interaction and relationships (Caberera et al., 1999; Pascarella & Terenzini, 1980; Tinto, 1975, 1993; Wood & Williams, 2013).

The benefits of having people in their institutions with whom they can relate on a fundamental level should not be overlooked. Black males complete postsecondary degrees at a lower rate than other groups (McFarland et al., 2018). Of those that endeavor to do so, some are also fathers, often because they may pursue higher education at a later age than the typical college student, after they have begun families, or as this study demonstrates, even *because* they have families. The continuing practices of community colleges having few to no Black men in academic and leadership roles need to change. Strategically planned outreach, marketing, and recruitment will arguably help alleviate the trend of low completion rates for impact Black male students, and by default, Black student-fathers, as these students will experience the college campus as a place they belong and where they can succeed.

Black student-fathers need to establish their own presence on campus. Based on the results of this study, it should not be left solely to community college administrators, faculty, and staff to recognize Black student-fathers. Black student-fathers should not feel that they need to remain idle in hopes of being acknowledged by others on campus. As previously stated, the noncognitve domain includes self-efficacy, sense of belonging, and identity (Wood & Harris, 2012). This means that Black student-fathers can exercise their self-efficacy to represent themselves.

To contribute to being recognized on community college campuses, Black student-fathers should seek assistance from their student government to start a club. A Black student-fathers club would not only establish a presence, but it would provide funding for events, awareness, and outreach. This would open opportunities for the recruitment of new and incoming Black student-fathers. An organization created by and featuring Black student-fathers would also give new and existing Black student-fathers extra support during their time at the institution.

Black student-fathers should also seek out and utilize the deans of students at their institutions. Working collaboratively with the deans will result in Black student-fathers' involvement and representation in decision-making processes. Social integration is key to persistence in higher education (Tinto, 1975; Mason, 1998; Wood & Harris, 2012). The partnership will help Black student-fathers create their own sense of belonging on community college campuses. Social integration on college campuses includes things such as group associations, interactions with college personnel, and involvement in extracurricular activities (Tinto, 1975). Successful interactions in these situations increase the likelihood of student persistence (Tinto, 1975). Black student-fathers speaking up for themselves and initiating their own campus activities will provide administrators, faculty, and staff with ideas and the understanding that they are a population in need of recognition and support.

RECOMMENDATIONS FOR FUTURE RESEARCH

This study examined how Black fathers' perceptions of their own and their father's fatherhood impact persistence in community college using a transcendental phenomenology framework. Continuing research on how fatherhood impacts persistence in higher education will contribute a deeper understanding and insight into our body of knowledge on this topic.

Broaden research nationally. Based on the results of this study, future qualitative studies might consider expanding the population to a larger geographic area. Based on the minimal amount of empirical studies on Black male retention in community colleges, and the disparity in college completion rates of Black males, there appears to be a need for continued research on Black student-fathers specifically, and Black male persistence overall (Harris & Wood, 2013; Mason, 1994, 1998; Wood & Turner, 2011). As community colleges are a valuable resource for people pursuing higher education without a family history of postsecondary education and those from lower-income brackets, a demographic many Black men are from, more studies of Black student-fathers in community colleges, given their particular relationship with the surrounding community, is especially important. Adding to the minimal literature that focuses on Black male education and fatherhood, and the intersections between them, is critical for the sake of future generations and their access to education and other opportunities. Further examination into possible solutions to improving the academic success rates for Black males could also highlight ways to increase opportunities for upward economic mobility of Black males through postsecondary education attainment.

Include 4-year institutions. Based on the findings of this study, the researcher recommends expanding the inquiry to 4-year colleges. The benefits of giving Black student-fathers a voice and an opportunity to be recognized can assist with retention and persistence efforts of Black males.

Examine student-fathers of different races. Future studies might examine how male participants of different races perceive their own and their father's fatherhood and how it impacts persistence in community college. The data would yield opportunities for comparisons between Black student-fathers and student-fathers of other racial backgrounds, as well as discern what might be universal concerns and challenges for student-fathers as a group.

LIMITATIONS

This section describes the limitations of the study that may impact the results and findings. First, the scope of the study was limited to nontraditional Black student-fathers in community colleges in New York State. Thus, any generalizations that may be inferred are limited to this population in this geographic region.

A second limitation is that some of the findings refer to fatherhood in general, as opposed to Black fatherhood specifically. The existence of more programs in community colleges for student-mothers than student-fathers is not specific to Black student-fathers. The concerns of Black student-fathers may be conflated with the concerns of student-fathers in general.

CONCLUSION

Despite an increase in nationwide postsecondary degree attainment, Black males still have the lowest percentage of earned postsecondary degrees in comparison to their White, Latinx and Asian counterparts (McFarland et al., 2018). Research shows a correlation between the lack of college degree attainment and lower socioeconomic status (Mirowsky & Ross, 2003; Palmer et al., 2014; Vuolo et al., 2016). Lower socioeconomic status has links to poorer health, unemployment, and incarceration rates. Several studies examine the challenges Black men face in American society, including numbers of lack of involvement as fathers (Beauchamps et al., 2018; Reynolds, 2009; Wilson et al., 2016). The importance of community colleges is highly recognized (AACC, 2020; Melguizo et al., 2013; O'Banion, 2013).

The purpose of this study was to gain a better understanding of how Black males experience their own and their father's fatherhood and the impact that it has, or has had, on their persistence in community college. The study utilized a three-pronged approach: the interstices between higher education, fatherhood, and being a Black man in the United States. The study also sought to learn more about whether Black student-fathers feel supported in community colleges and how community colleges provide resources to foster this student population's success. The study also aimed to give Black student-fathers a voice to speak directly to these experiences.

This study addressed three key concerns: (a) some U.S. citizens are living in poverty largely due to their lack of postsecondary education credentials (O'Banion, 2013; Carnevale et al., 2011), (b) close to 99% of the jobs added after the recession went to employees who had postsecondary education (Carnevale et al., 2016), and (c) Black males have the lowest percentage of earned postsecondary degrees in comparison to males from other ethnic groups (NCES, 2018). These facts matter because health concerns, unemployment, poverty, and incarceration rates are inversely correlated with earned college degrees and subsequent higher socioeconomic status (Mirowsky & Ross, 2003; Palmer et al., 2014; Vuolo et al., 2016). These outcomes can have profound outcomes in terms of family structures, economic resources, parental availability, and intergenerational pursuit of and access to higher education, and the concomitant benefits these confer on society at large (e.g., increased tax revenues, lower crime rates, lower incarceration rates, lower child poverty rates, more psychologically and emotionally stable children).

The research paradigm of this study was a transcendental phenomenological design that assisted the researcher in exploring the phenomenon of the lived experiences of Black student-fathers in community colleges. Through semistructured interviews, the overall essence of the "what" and the "how" of the phenomenon was taken from the textural-structural synthesis of participants' lived experiences (Moustakas, 1994) and expressed through three key findings.

First, fatherhood acts as a catalyst to community college completion for Black student-fathers. This finding emerged from the research question, "How do Black male college students experience fatherhood (from a son's perspective) facilitating or impeding community college completion?" The theme was parenting matters, with subthemes of healthy parenting and unhealthy parenting.

The second finding was that children are at the center of persistence for Black student-fathers. This finding emerged from the research question, "How do Black male college students experience fatherhood (from a father's perspective) facilitating or or impeding community college completion?" The themes were impenetrable lifelong connection, resilience and progress, and desire to be living proof.

The third finding was support systems in community colleges are lacking for Black student-fathers. This finding emerged from the research question "In the experience of Black male college students, how do community colleges support Black students who are fathers?" The themes were typical unnecessary obstacles and true acknowledgment and acceptance with the subthemes lack of support and racism.

Based on the findings of the study, it is apparent that Black student-fathers in community colleges will continue to feel invisible and unsupported until changes are made by the campus community, beginning with the administrators. It is known that Black male persistence in higher education is low, owing to a myriad of factors. Some of these students are also fathers. Along with their status as Black men, their fatherhood is the most powerful defining aspect of their existence.

As evidenced in this study, their children have been larger supports for their persistence through the completion of their academic programs than the institutions in which they are enrolled. If community colleges examine the evidence provided in this study and sincerely want to help Black student-fathers establish visibility and presence as fellow students in the larger campus community, which is comprised of people from all walks and circumstances of life, they will need to recognize them as a relevant student population, provide specific support programs for them, and make a concerted effort to employ people like them in faculty, support staff, and administrative roles. A greater understanding of the role of community college completion in family structure and success, as well as the impediments to completing such degrees, are critical to pursuing equity in a population that has historically suffered disproportionate disadvantage and limited opportunities. The existing data on Black male completion of postsecondary education shows that the current status quo does not achieve what is necessary for maximizing the opportunities for citizens to reach their highest potential professionally and academically achieve the American Dream.

It is the researcher's hope that this study serves as evidence—indeed, living proof—that negative stereotypes must be actively confronted and deconstructed when we think about Black fathers. The stereotypes must not be the default. That narrative must change as it diminishes the countless Black fathers who possess the drive to be successful in education, fatherhood, and in their lives, often against formidable structural barriers. This is their ambition whether or not they had involved fathers themselves. The participants in this study decided to take their collective history into their hands and reshape it into a better future for themselves, but mostly, and ultimately, for the sake of their children: their posterity and society's future.

REFERENCES

Abrutyn, S., & Mueller, A. S. (2014). The socioemotional foundations of suicide: A microsociological view of Durkheim's suicide. *Sociological Theory, 32*(4), 327–351.

Adams, C. J. (2012). 'Soft skills' seen as key element for higher ed. *Education Week, 32*(12), 1-1, 14.

Alexander, M. (2012). *The new Jim Crow: Mass incarceration in the age of colorblindness* (Rev. ed.). New York, NY: New Press.

Aljohani, O. (2016). A review of the contemporary international literature on student retention in higher education. *International Journal of Education & Literacy Studies, 4*(1), 40-52.

Allen, M. (2016). Processes of racialization through media depictions of transracial violence. *Undergraduate Review, 12*, 7-18.

Allen, Q. (2015). "Tell your own story": Manhood, masculinity and racial socialization among Black fathers and their sons. *Ethnic and Racial Studies*, *39*(10), 1831–1848.

Altbach, P., Berdahl, R., & Gumport, P. (2011). *American higher education in the twenty-first century: Social, political, and economic challenges.* (3rd ed.) Baltimore, MD: Johns Hopkins University Press

American Association of Community Colleges. (2012, April). Reclaiming the American dream: A report from the 21st-century commission on the future of community colleges. Washington, DC: Author.

American Association of Community Colleges. (2020). Data points: More education = Better jobs. Retrieved from https://www.aacc.nche.edu

Anumba, E. (2015). Successfully navigating through college: Voices of African American males. *International Journal of Teacher Leadership*, *1*(6), 35–56.

Assari, S., Thomas, A., Caldwell, C., & Mincy, R. (2017). Blacks' diminished health return of family structure and socioeconomic status; 15 years of follow-up of a national urban sample of youth. *Journal of Urban Health*, *95*(1), 21–35.

Association of American Colleges and Universities. (n.d.). Retrieved from https://www.aacu.org/aacu-news/newsletter/facts-figures/jan-feb2017

Astin, A. W. (1975). *Preventing students from dropping out*. San Francisco, CA: Jossey- Bass.

Astin, A. W. (1984). Student involvement: A developmental theory for higher education. *Journal of College Student Personnel, 25*(4), 297– 308.

Bandura, A. (1977). Self-efficacy: Toward a unifying theory of behavioral change. *Psychological Review, 84*(2), 191-215.

Bean, J. (1980). Dropouts and turnover: The synthesis and test of a causal model of student attrition. *Research in Higher Education, 12*(2), 155-187.

Bean, J. (1983). The application of a model of turnover in work organizations to the student attrition process. *Review of Higher Education, 6(2),* 129-148.

Bean, J. P., & Metzner, B. S. (1985). A conceptual model of nontraditional student attrition. *Review of Educational Research, 55*(4), 485-540.

Beauchamp, A., Sanzenbacher, G., Seitz, S., & Skira, M. (2014). *Deadbeat dads. Boston College Working Papers in Economics No. 859*, Boston, MA: Boston College.

Beauchamp, A., Sanzenbacher, G., Seitz, S., & Skira, M. (2018). Single moms and deadbeat dads: The role of earnings, marriage market conditions, and preference heterogeneity. *International Economic Review, 59*(1), 191–232.

Bellagamba, A., Greene, S., Klein, M., & Brown, C. (2013). *African voices on slavery and the slave trade.* Cambridge, England: Cambridge University Press.

Berger, J., Ramirez, G. B., & Lyon, S. (2012). *Past to present: A historical look at retention. In A. Seidman (Ed.), College student retention: Formula for student success* (pp. 7-34). Rowman & Littlefield.

Bird, C., Seeman, T., Escarce, J., Basurto-Dávila, R., Finch, B., Dubowitz, T., Heron, M., Hale, L., Merkin, S., Weden, M., & Lurie, N. (2010). Neighbourhood socioeconomic status and biological "wear and tear" in a nationally representative sample of US adults. *Journal of Epidemiology and Community Health (1979), 64*(10), 860–865.

Bobo, L & Thompson, V. (2010). *Racialized mass incarceration: Poverty, prejudice, and punishment.* In H. R. Markus and P. M. L. Moya (Eds.), Doing race: 21 essays for the 21st century, (pp. 322-355). New York, NY: Norton.

Boyd, H. (2016, Aug). Alexander Twilight, the first African-American college graduate in US. *New York*

Amsterdam News Retrieved from http://amsterdamnews.com/news/2016/aug/04/alexander-twilight-first-african-american-college-/

Boyd, T., & Mitchell, D. (2018). Black male persistence in spite of facing stereotypes in college: A phenomenological exploration. *The Qualitative Report, 23*(4), 893-913.

Brand, J., Pfeffer, F., & Goldrick-Rab, S. (2014). The community college effect revisited: The importance of attending to heterogeneity and complex counterfactuals. *Sociological Science, 1*(25), 448-465.

Brito, T. (2012). Fathers behind bars: Rethinking child support policy toward low-income noncustodial fathers and their families. *Journal of Gender, Race, and Justice, 15*, 617–689.

Bronfenbrenner, U. (1996). *The ecology of human development experiments by nature and design.* Cambridge, MA: Harvard University Press.

Brooks, J. (2015). The impact of family Structure, relationships, and support on African American students' collegiate experiences. *Journal of Black Studies, 46*(8), 817-836.

Bungay, V., Oliffe, J., & Atchison, C. (2016). Addressing underrepresentation in sex work research: Reflections on designing a purposeful sampling strategy. *Qualitative Health Research, 26*(7), 966–978.

Bush, E. C., & Bush, L. (2010). Calling out the elephant: An examination of African American male achievement in community colleges. *Journal of African American Males in Education, 1*(1), 40-62.

Cabrera. A, & Nora, A. (1994). College student's perceptions of prejudice and discrimination and their feelings of alienation: A construct validation approach. *Review of Education, Pedagogy, and Cultural Studies, 16*(3), 387-409.

Cabrera, A., Nora, A., Castañeda, M., & Hengstler, D. (1992). The role of finances in the persistence process: A structural model. *Research in Higher Education, 33*(5), 571-593.

Cabrera, A., Nora, A., & Castañeda, M., & Hengstler, D. (1993). College persistence. *The Journal of Higher Education, 64* (2), 123-139

Cabrera, A., Nora, A., Terenzini, P., Pascarella, E., & Hagedorn, L. (1999). Campus racial climate and the adjustment of students to college: A comparison between White students and African-American students. *The Journal of Higher Education, 70*(2), 134–160.

Carnevale, A., Rose, S., & Cheah, B. (2011). *The undereducated American.* Washington, DC: Georgetown University Center on Education and the Workforce.

Carnevale, A. P., Smith, N. & Strohl, J. (2013). *Recovery: Job growth and educational requirements through 2020.* Washington, DC: Georgetown University Center on Education and the Workforce. Retrieved from https://cew.georgetown.edu/cew-reports/recovery-job-growth-and-education-requirements-through-2020/

Carnevale, A. P., Jayasundera, T. & Gulish, A. (2016). *America's divided recovery.* Retrieved from https://cew.georgetown.edu/cew-reports/americas-divided-recovery/.

Choi, J., & Jackson, A. (2011). Fathers' involvement and child behavior problems in poor African American single-mother families. *Children and Youth Services Review, 33*(5), 698–704.

Conlin, M. (2015). *One nation divided by slavery: Remembering the American revolution while marching toward the civil war.* Kent, OH: Kent State University Press.

Connor, M., & White, J. (2011). *Black fathers: An invisible presence in America* (2nd ed.). New York, NY: Routledge.

Cooper, S., Burnett, M., Johnson, M., Brooks, J., Shaheed, J., & McBride, M. (2020). "That is why we raise children": African American fathers' race-related concerns for their adolescents and parenting strategies. *Journal of Adolescence, 82,* 67–81.

Cooper, F. (2013). We are always already imprisoned: Hyperincarceration and Black male identity performance. *Boston University Law Review, 93*(3) 1185–1204.

Creswell, J.W. & Poth, C. N. (2018). *Qualitative inquiry & research design* (5th ed.). Thousand Oaks, CA: Sage Publications.

Crisp, G., & Cruz, I. (2009). Mentoring college students: A critical review of the literature between 1990 and 2007. *Research in Higher Education, 50*(6), 525-545.

Cross, W. E., Jr., Parham, T. A., & Helms, J. E. (1991). *The stages of Black identity development: Nigrescence models.* In R. L. Jones (Ed.), *Black psychology* (pp. 319–338). Hampton, VA: Cobb & Henry Publishers.

Cross, C. (1999). *Justin Smith Morrill: Father of the land-grant colleges.* East Lansing, MI: Michigan State University Press.

Department of Education. (1964). Education and Title VI. Retrieved from https://www2.ed.gov/ about/ offices/ list/ocr/docs/hq43e4.html Demetriou, C. & Schmitz-Sciborski, A. (2011). Integration, motivation, strengths and optimism: Retention theories past. present and future. In R. Hayes (Ed.), *Proceedings of the 7th*

National Symposium on Student Retention, (pp. 300-312). Norman, OK: The University of Oklahoma Press.

Du Bois, W. E. B. (1903) *The souls of Black folk.* Chicago, IL: A.C. McClurg & Co.

Duncan, G., Magnuson, K., Votruba-Drzal, E., (2014). Boosting family income to promote child development. *The Future of Children, 24*(1), 99–120.

Duque, V., Pilkauskas, N., & Garfinkel, I. (2018). Assets among low-income families in the Great Recession. *PloS One, 13*(2), e0192370.

Durkheim, E. 2005. *On Suicide: A study in sociology.* New York, NY: Routledge.Finlay, L. (2009). Debating phenomenological research methods. *Phenomenology and Practice, 3*(1), 6-25.

Fornili, K.S. (2018). Racialized mass incarceration and the war on drugs: A critical race theory appraisal. *Journal of Addictions Nursing, 29*(1), 65-72.

Foster, T. (2011). The sexual abuse of black men under American slavery. *Journal of the History of Sexuality, 20*(3), 445–464.

Glenn, F. (2003). The retention of Black male students in Texas public community colleges. *Journal of College Student Retention, 5*(2), 115–133.

Goldrick-Rab, S. (2010). Challenges and opportunities for improving community college student success. *Review of Educational Research, 80*(3), 437–469.

Goldrick-Rab, S., & Pfeffer, F. 2009. Beyond access: Explaining social class differences in college student mobility. *Sociology of Education, 82*(2), 101–125.

Gordon, T., Nichter, M., & Henriksen, R. (2013). Raising Black males from a Black father's perspective: A phenomenological study. *The Family Journal, 21*(2), 154–161.

Gumperz, J. (1977). The sociolinguistic significance of conversational code-switching. *RELC Journal, 8*(2), 1-34.

Guryan, J. (2004). Desegregation and Black dropout rates. *The American Economic Review, 94*(4), 919–943.

Gutman, H. (1976). *The Black family in slavery and freedom, 1750-1925* (1st ed.). New York, NY: Pantheon Books.

Hagedorn, L., Maxwell, W., & Hampton, P. (2001). Correlates of retention for African-American males in community colleges. *Journal of College Student Retention, 3*(3), 243–263.

Harper, S. R. (2008). Realizing the intended outcomes of Brown: High achieving African American male undergraduates and social capital. *American Behavioral Scientist, 51*(7), 1029-1052.

Harper, S. R. (2012). *Black, male student success in higher education: A report from the national Black, male college achievement study.* Philadelphia, PA: University of Pennsylvania, Center for the Study of Race and Equity in Education. Retrieved from https://webapp.usc.edu/web/rossier/publications/231/Harper%20(2012)%20Black%20Male%20Success.pdf

Harris, F. III, & Wood, J. L. (2013). Student success for men of color in community colleges: A review of published literature and research, 1998–2012. *Journal of Diversity in Higher Education, 6*(3), 174–185.

Harris, F., & Luke Wood, J. (2016). Applying the socio-ecological outcomes model to the student experiences of men of color. *New Directions for Community Colleges, 174,* 35-46.

Helms, J. E. (Ed.). (1990). *Black and White racial identity: Theory, research, and practice.* Santa Barbara, CA: Greenwood Press.

Herr, R., Bosch, J., Loerbroks, A., van Vianen, A., Jarczok, M., Fischer, J., & Schmidt, B. (2015). Three job stress models and their relationship with musculoskeletal pain in blue- and white-collar workers. *Journal of Psychosomatic Research, 79*(5), 340–347

Holliday, C., & Strange, N. Y. (2013). The lived experiences of African American males in an urban university setting. In M. S. Plakhotnik & S. M. Nielsen (Eds.), *Proceedings of the 12th Annual South Florida Education Research Conference* (pp. 116-123). Miami, FL: Florida International University.

Hummer, R.A., & Lariscy, J.T. (2011). Educational attainment and adult mortality. *International Handbook of Adult Mortality*, 2, 241-61.

Jackson, H., & Jackson, K. (2016). We are family: I got all my (HBCU) Sisters with me. *Composition Studies*, 44(2), 153–157.

Joreskog, K.G. & Sorbom, B. (1988). PRELIS: A program for multivariate data screening and data summarization (2nd ed.). Mooresville, IN: Scientific Software.

Joreskog, K.G. & Sorbom, B. (1993). LISREL 8. Hillsdale, NJ: Lawrence Erlbaum Associates.

Karls, J. M., Lowery, C. T., Mattaini, M. A., & Wandrei, K. E. (1997). The use of the pie (person-in-environment) system in social work education. *Journal of Social Work Education*, 33(1), 49–58.

Kleider-Offutt, H., Bond, A., & Hegerty, S. (2017). Black stereotypical features: When a face type can get you in trouble. *Current Directions in Psychological Science*, 26(1), 28-33.

Knaggs, C., Sondergeld, T., & Schardt, B. (2015). Overcoming barriers to college enrollment, persistence, and perceptions for urban high school students in a college preparatory program. *Journal of Mixed Methods Research, 9*(1), 7-30.

Lemmons, B., & Johnson, W. (2019). Game changers: A critical race theory analysis of the economic, social, and political factors impacting Black fatherhood and family formation. *Social Work in Public Health: Race and Social Policy, 34*(1), 86–101.

Lent, R., Brown, S., & Larkin, K. (1986). Self-efficacy in the prediction of academic performance and perceived career options. *Journal of Counseling Psychology, 33*(3), 265–269.

Levin, J.S., Haberler, Z, Walker, L. & Jackson-Boothby, A. (2014). Community college culture and faculty of color. *Community College Review, 42*(1), 55-74.

Longwell-Grice, R., & Longwell-Grice, H. (2007). Testing Tinto: How do retention theories work for first-generation, working-class students? *Journal of College Student Retention: Research, Theory and Practice, 9*(4), 407-420

Mangan, K. (2014). Minority male students face challenge to achieve at community colleges. *The Chronicle of Higher Education, 60*(25), 5.

Maslow, A. H. (1943). A theory of human motivation. *Psychological Review, 50*(4), 370–396.

Mason, H. (1994). *The relationships of academic, background, and environmental variables in the persistence of adult African American male students in an urban community college* (doctoral dissertation.) Retrieved from ProQuest Dissertations and Theses.

Mason, H. P. (1998). A persistence model for African American male urban community college students. *Community College Journal of Research & Practice, 22*(8), 751-761.

McFarland, J., Hussar, B., Wang, X., Zhang, J., Wang, K., Rathbun, A., Barmer, A.,Forrest Cataldi, E., and Bullock Mann, F. (2018). *The Condition of Education 2018 (NCES 2018-144)*. U.S. Department of Education. Washington, DC: National Center for Education Statistics. Retrieved from https://nces.ed.gov/pubsearch/pubsinfo.as/?pubid=2018144

McNelis, A. (2017). Habitually offending the constitution: The cruel and unusual consequences of habitual offender laws and mandatory minimums. *George Mason University Civil Rights Law Journal, 28*(1), 97-126.

Melguizo, T., Kienzl, G., & Kosiewicz, H. (2013). The potential of community colleges to increase Bachelor's degree attainment rates. In L. W. Perna & A.

P. Jones (Eds.), *The tate of college access and completion* (pp. 140-165). New York, NY: Routledge.

Metz, G. (2004). Challenge and changes to Tinto's persistence theory: A historical review. *Journal of College Student Retention, 6*(2), 191-207.

Mirowsky, J., & Ross, C.E. (2003). *Education, social status, and health* Hawthorne, NY: Aldine de Gruyter.

Moody, J. (2001). Race, School Integration, and Friendship Segregation in America. *The American Journal of Sociology, 107*(3), 679–716.

Moss, H. (2007). New Haven's ill-fated attempt to establish the first Black college. *The Journal of Blacks in Higher Education, 58,* 78–79.

Moustakas, C. E. (1994). *Phenomenological research methods.* Thousand Oaks, CA:Sage Publications.

Musu-Gillette, L., de Brey, C., McFarland, J., Hussar, W., Sonnenberg, W., & Wilkinson-Flicker, S. (2017). Status and trends in the education of racial and ethnic groups. Retrieved from https://nces.ed.gov/pubs2017/2017051.pdf

Mwangi, C., Thelamour, B., Ezeofor, I., & Carpenter, A. (2018). "Black elephant in the room": Black students contextualizing campus racial climate within US racial climate. *Journal of College Student Development, 59*(4), 456–474.

National Fatherhood Initiative. (2018). Retrieved from https://www.fatherhood.org/

National Center for Education Statistics. (2019). *Digest of education statistics.* Retrieved from https://nces.ed.gov/programs/digest/d19/tables/dt19_321.20.asp

National Urban League. (2014). From access to completion: A seamless path to college graduation for African American students. Retrieved from http://nulwb.iamempowered.com/research/access-completion-seamless-path-college-completion-african-americans

Nora, A., & Cabrera, A. (1996). The role of perceptions of prejudice and discrimination on the adjustment of minority students to college. *The Journal of Higher Education, 67*(2), 119–148.

O'Banion, T. (2013). *Access, success, and completion. A primer for community college faculty, administrators, trustees, and staff.* Chandler, AZ: League for Innovation in the Community College.

Orrock, J., & Clark, M. (2018). Using systems theory to promote academic success for African American males. *Urban Education, 53*(8), 1013-1042.

Padilla-Díaz, M. (2015). Phenomenology in educational qualitative research: Philosophy as science or philosophical science? *International Journal of Educational Excellence, 1*(2), 101–110.

Palmer, R., Wood, J., Dancy, T., & Strayhorn, T. (2014). Black male collegians: Increasing access, retention, and persistence in higher education. Appendix. *ASHE Higher Education Report, 40*(3), 1-147.

Parham, T. A., & Helms, J. E. (1981). The influence of Black students' racial identity attitudes on preferences for counselor's race. *Journal of Counseling Psychology, 28*(3), 250–257.

Pascarella, E. T. (1980). Student-faculty informal contact and college outcomes. *Review of Educational Research, 50*(4), 545–595.

Pascarella, E., & Terenzini, P. (1979). Student-faculty informal contact and college persistence: A further investigation. *The Journal of Educational Research, 72*(4), 214–218.

Pascarella, E., & Terenzini, P. (1980). Predicting freshman persistence and voluntary dropout decisions from a theoretical model. *The Journal of Higher Education, 51*(1), 60–75.

Pascarella, E. T., & Terenzini, P. T. (1983). Predicting voluntary freshman year persistence/withdrawal behavior in a residential university: A path analytic validation of Tinto's model. *Journal of Educational Psychology, 75*(2), 215–226.

Pascarella, E. T., & Terenzini, P. T. (1991). How college affects students: Findings and Insights from twenty years of research. San Francisco, CA: Jossey-Bass.

Prison Policy Initiative. (2017). Retrieved from https://www.prisonpolicy.org/reports/money.html

Randolph, A. (2010). Black codes. In K. Lomotey (Ed.), *Encyclopedia of African American education* (pp. 75-76). Thousand Oaks, CA: Sage Publications.

Reid, K. (2013). Understanding the relationships among racial identity, self-efficacy, institutional integration and academic achievement of Black males attending research universities. *The Journal of Negro Education, 82*(1), 75–93.

Reynolds, T. (2009). Exploring the absent/present dilemma: Black fathers, family relationships, and social capital in Britain. *The Annals of the American Academy of Political and Social Science, 624*(1), 12–28.

Rhoden. (2017). "Trust me, you are going to college": How trust influences academicachievement in Black males. *The Journal of Negro Education, 86*(1), 52–64.

Roberts, D. (2004). The social and moral cost of mass incarceration in African American communities. *Stanford Law Review, 56*(5), 1271-1305.

Seidman, A. (2012). *College student retention: Formula for student success.* Lanham, MA: Rowman & Littlefield.

Schafer, M., Wilkinson, L., & Ferraro, K. (2013). Childhood (mis)fortune, educational attainment, and adult health: Contingent benefits of a college degree? *Social Forces, 91*(3), 1007-1034.

Smiley, C., & Fakunle, D. (2016). From "brute" to "thug:" The demonization and criminalization of unarmed Black male victims in America. *Journal of Human Behavior in the Social Environment, 26*(3-4), 350–366.

Smith, P., Ralph, J. R., LaFayette, B., & Finley, M. L. (2016). *The Chicago freedom movement: Martin Luther King, Jr. And civil rights activism in the north.* Lexington, KY: University Press of Kentucky.

Sowell, T. (2018). *Discrimination and disparities.* New York, NY: Basic Books.

Spady, W. (1970). Dropouts from higher education: An interdisciplinary review and synthesis. *Interchange, 1*(1), 64-85.

Strauss, A., & Corbin, J. (1998). *Basics of qualitative research: Techniques and procedures for developing grounded theory* (2nd ed.). Thousand Oaks, CA: Sage.

Strayhorn, T. L. (2008). The role of supportive relationships in facilitating African American males' success in college. *NASPA Journal, 45*(1), 26-48.

Strayhorn, T. L. (2012). Satisfaction and retention among African American men at two-year community colleges. *Community College Journal of Research and Practice, 36*(5), 358-375.

Strayhorn, T. (2014). Making a way to success: Self-authorship and academic achievement of first-year African American students at historically Black colleges. *Journal of College Student Development, 55*(2), 151–167.

Strayhorn, T. (2015). Introduction: A special issue of Spectrum: A journal on Black men. *Spectrum: A Journal on Black Men, 4*(1), 1-4.

Strayhorn, T., Hilton, A., & Bonner, F. (2017). Factors that influence the persistence and success of Black men in urban public universities. *Urban Education, 52*(9), 1106-1128.

Sutton, J. (2013). Symbol and substance: Effects of California's three strikes law on felony sentencing. *Law & Society Review, 47*(1), 37–72.

Teasley, M., Schiele, J., Adams, C., & Okilwa, N. (2018). Trayvon Martin: Racial profiling, Black male stigma, and social work practice. *Social Work, 63*(1), 37–46.

Teh, Y., & Lek, E. (2018). Culture and reflexivity: systemic journeys with a British Chinese family. *Journal of Family Therapy, 40*(4), 520–536.

Temin, P. (2017). *The vanishing middle class: Prejudice and power in a dual economy.* Cambridge, MA: MIT Press.

Teranishi, R., Behringer, L., Grey, E., & Parker, T. (2009). Critical race theory and research on Asian Americans and Pacific Islanders in higher education. *New Directions for Institutional Research, 142,* 57–68.

Thibodeau, L., & Lachaud, J. (2016). Impact of economic fluctuations on suicide mortality in Canada (1926–2008): Testing the Durkheim, Ginsberg, and Henry and short theories. *Death Studies, 40*(5), 1-11.

Tierney, W. G. (1992). An anthropological analysis of student participation in college. *Journal of Higher Education, 63*(6), 603-618.

Tinto, V. (1975). Dropout from higher education: A theoretical synthesis of recent research. *Review of Educational Research, 45*(1), 89-125.

Tinto, V. (1993). *Leaving college: Rethinking the causes and cures of student attrition.* (2nd ed.). Chicago, IL: University of Chicago Press.

Tinto, V. (2012). *Completing college: Rethinking institutional action*. Chicago, IL: University of Chicago Press.

Tolliver, D., & Miller, M. (2018). Graduation 101: Critical strategies for African American men college completion. *Education, 138*(4), 301-308.

U.S. Department of Education. (2011, March). *Meeting the nation's 2020 goal: State targets for increasing the number and percentage of college graduates with degrees*. Washington, D.C. Retrieved from http://www.Whitehouse.gov/ sites/default/files/completion_state_by_state.pdf

U.S. Department of Education. (1991). *Historically Black colleges and universities and higher education desegregation*. Washington, D.C. Retrieved from https://www2.ed.gov/about/offices/list/ocr/docs/hq9511.html

Vasquez Urias, M., & Wood, J. (2014). Black male graduation rates in community colleges: Do institutional characteristics make a difference? *Community College Journal of Research and Practice, 38*(12), 1112–1124.

Vuolo, M., Mortimer, J., & Staff, J. (2016). The value of educational degrees in turbulent economic times: Evidence from the youth development study. *Social Science Research, 57*, 233-252.

Wilson, A., Henriksen, R., Bustamante, R., & Irby, B. (2016). Successful Black men from absent-father homes and their resilient single mothers: A phenomenological study. *Journal of Multicultural Counseling and Development, 44*(3), 189–208.

Wood, J. L. (2011, August 5). Laying the groundwork— Black male programs and initiatives in community colleges. *Community College Times.*

Wood, J. L. (2013). The same . . . but different: Examining background characteristics among Black males in public two-year colleges. *Journal of Negro Education, 82*(1), 47–61.

Wood, J. (2014). Examining academic variables affecting the persistence and attainment of Black male collegians: A focus on academic performance and integration in the two-year college. *Race, Ethnicity, and Education, 17*(5), 601-622.

Wood, J. L., & Harris, F., III. (2012, November). Examining factors that influence men of color's success in community colleges. Paper presented at the annual meeting of the Council on Ethnic Participation, Association for the Study of Higher Education, Las Vegas, NV.

Wood, J., & Harrison, J. (2014). College choice for Black males in the community college: Factors influencing institutional selection. *Negro Educational Review, 65*(1-4), 87-97.

Wood, J. L., Hilton, A. A., & Lewis, C. (2011). Black male collegians in public two-year colleges: Student perspectives on the effect of employment on academic success. *National Association of Student Affairs Professionals Journal, 14*(1), 97-110.

Wood, J. L. & Turner, C. S.V. (2011). Black males and the community college: Student perspectives on faculty and academic success. *Community College Journal of Research & Practice, 35,* 135-151.

Wood, J., & Williams, R. (2013). Persistence factors for Black males in the community college: An examination of background, academic, social, and environmental variables. S*pectrum: A Journal on Black Men, 1*(2), 1-28

Yosso, T. (2005). Whose culture has capital? A critical race theory discussion of community cultural wealth. *Race, Ethnicity, and Education, 8*(1), 69-91.

Zamani-Gallaher, E. (2010). *Higher education act of 1965.* In K. Lomotey (Ed.), *Encyclopedia of African American education* (pp. 312-315). Thousand Oaks, CA: Sage.

Zhao, Feng, & Carlos Castillo-Chavez. (2014). The dynamics of poverty and crime.

Journal of Shanghai Normal University (Natural Sciences), 43(5), 486–495.

APPENDIX A

BLACK STUDENT FATHER PERSISTENCE QUESTIONNAIRE:

Please answer the following questions:

Demographics:

(1) Name: _____

(2) What is your racial identity (ex. Black, African American, etc.)? _____

(3) Age: _____

(4) How many children do you have? _____

(5) What is your enrollment status (Full-Time or Part-Time)? _____

(6) What degree or certificate program are you in?
_____

(7) What is your current GPA? _____

(8) When did you begin at your institution?
_____

(9) How are you paying for classes?
_____

(10) Have you participated in any campus activities (athletics, student government, etc.)? _____

(11) If yes, which ones?
_____

(12) What is your current employment status?
_____

(13) What are your living arrangements with your child(ren)?_____

(14) What is your relationship status with the mother(s) of your child(ren)?
_____

(15) What best describes your father's career? (Check all that apply)

___ In and out of work ___ Steady employment
___ Unemployed

___ I don't know   ___ Other (Please Explain)
_____

(16) What best describes your father's education? (Check all that apply)

___ 8th grade or less   ___ High School

___ Associate's Degree

___ Bachelor's Degree ___ Master's Degree

___ Doctoral Degree

___ I don't know   ___ Other (Please Explain)

www.ingramcontent.com/pod-product-compliance
Lightning Source LLC
Chambersburg PA
CBHW020839160426
43192CB00007B/711